Unlawful Killing

Unlawful Killing

Judith Cook

BLOOMSBURY

Acknowledgements

Unlike my early material on Hilda Murrell, this book is not just the result of my own personal research. A good many people assisted me by pooling what they knew. As not all of them wished to be acknowledged by name, I have decided not to identify anyone. I would just like to express my gratitude to all concerned.

I would like to thank my agent, Bill Hamilton, for his support and also David Reynolds of Bloomsbury Publishing.

First published in Great Britain 1994
Bloomsbury Publishing Plc, 2 Soho Square, London W1V 5DE

Copyright © 1994 by Judith Cook

The moral right of the author has been asserted

PICTURE SOURCES

Shropshire Star: pages 1–6
The Times: page 7 *top*
Yorkshire Post: page 7 *bottom*
Associated Press: page 8 *top*
Press Association: page 8 *bottom*

A CIP catalogue record for this book
is available from the British Library

ISBN 0 7475 1822 X

Typeset by Hewer Text Composition Services, Edinburgh
Printed in England by Clays Ltd, St Ives plc

'But that was in another country and besides, the wench is dead.'

Christopher Marlowe, *The Jew of Malta*

'Any man's death diminishes me, because I am involved in mankind.'

John Donne

Contents

Prologue

On the morning of Saturday 24 March 1984, the body of an elderly woman was found in a copse six miles outside Shrewsbury. She was half-naked and had superficial injuries. Later it would be said that the probable cause of death was hypothermia. The police concluded, after a lengthy investigation, that the woman's death was the result of a break-in by an opportunist burglar that had gone 'tragically wrong'. They have never deviated from that conclusion.

The woman's name was Hilda Murrell.

Her murderer has never been caught and the crime has passed into legend as one of the great unsolved mysteries of its decade; and not only in this country. In the United States they call her 'Britain's Karen Silkwood', a reference to the American woman who died in mysterious circumstances on her way to blow the whistle on unsafe practices in a nuclear plant.

Hilda Murrell died because she happened to be the wrong person in the wrong place at the wrong time.

On 8 May 1979 the Conservatives won the General Election following the notorious 'winter of discontent'. The victory ushered in a new Prime Minister who was to change the

1

political climate fundamentally and for ever. Clips of the film of Margaret Thatcher's first arrival at 10 Downing Street show the waiting, cheering crowd, the television reporter clutching his microphone and describing in hushed tones the arrival of the cavalcade of cars bearing the new incumbent; then the leading limousine draws to a halt and Margaret Thatcher steps out.

Her hair is neatly waved but has not acquired the height and rigidity it was later to assume, nor is her face stiff with the maquillage of later years. She wears a rather ordinary blue suit, with a pleated skirt, and a neat spotted blouse. She clutches an enormous handbag and her eyes gleam with the expression we were all to come to know and which was such a gift to cartoonists. Underneath the handles of the handbag, she is holding a card.

After expressing her delight at the election result and cutting through the questions of the interviewer in the way we would also learn to recognise, she reads from the card words which she attributes to St Francis of Assisi:

> Where there is discord, may we bring harmony,
> Where there is error, may we bring truth,
> Where there is doubt, may we bring faith,
> Where there is despair, may we bring hope.

The words are not those of St Francis, but a nineteenth-century pastiche.

PART I

The Killing I

Chapter 1

'A very private person . . .'

Hilda Murrell was born at Eaton Cottage in Shrewsbury on 3 February 1906, the elder daughter of Owen and Lily Murrell. She was, one might say, born into roses, for her father and his brother, Edwin, ran a famous rose nursery in the Belvedere area on the eastern outskirts of the town.

She did not, however, plan a career in horticulture. From Shrewsbury High School she won a scholarship to Newham College, Cambridge, where she read English, Modern and Medieval Languages, and French. She graduated in 1928. As was the case for women of a slightly earlier generation, such as Vera Brittain and Dorothy Sayers, the university still did not award degrees to women graduates. That had to come later.

Later she would confess to friends that she would have preferred an academic career and still hankered after it, but as there was no son or nephew to carry on the family firm, she felt it was only right that she should agree to do so and joined her father and uncle on coming down from Cambridge. She immediately set about learning the business with the energy and thoroughness which was her hallmark, so much so that she became an expert, a specialist in the growing of very old roses and miniatures, travelling Europe to find unusual species.

She became a supplier of roses to famous gardens from those of Buckingham Palace to that of Vita Sackville-West. She regularly took Gold Awards at all the major shows, including the Chelsea Flower Show and eventually had a rose named after her, a deep, clear pink described by rose-grower David Austin as having flowers that are 'very nearly perfect'.

She is variously described by those who came to know her in those days as 'a strong-minded woman', 'a woman of personal gentleness and great dedication' and 'a real lady of the old school'.

Hilda never married and there is no record that she was ever tempted to do so. Throughout her life she also had to battle with an inconvenient disability. Her right eye had been irreparably damaged in childhood following an infection, and she saw only with her left. She never got over being self-conscious about it and disliked being photographed. Some of those who knew her put her penchant for the large floppy hats in which she appears on the few photographs released after her death down to a desire to camouflage her blind eye. It did not, however, prevent her from following a wide range of interests: when she went bird-watching she simply used a small spy-glass instead of the usual 'twitchers' 'binoculars.

During the Second World War she worked with the Jewish Refugees' Children's Society to raise funds and help place children who had escaped the holocaust in suitable homes in Shropshire and the Welsh Marches.

At the end of the war, Owen Murrell died and Hilda's cousin, Leslie, joined her in the running of the nursery, although it was to remain under her sole management. In 1961 the land on which the nursery stood was wanted for the building of the new Shire Hall, so the cousins moved their operation out of the Column area to a new site next to the A5 by-pass, where it is clearly marked by a large sign which now reads 'Percy Thrower's Nursery'. A year later she helped found the Shropshire Conservation Trust (now the Shropshire Trust for Nature Conservation), on whose council she sat for many years. Her friend Charles Sinker, who edited her *Nature Diaries*,[1] published after her death, paints a picture of a woman who did not suffer fools gladly. 'She showed on occasion,' he says, 'an understandable impatience with the Trust for its slow progress over local conservation issues, and what she considered its timid, parochial and ultra-diplomatic attitude on matters of wider importance. She gave forthright voice to her feelings, while remaining a loyal member.' Later she was to find the Shropshire branch of the Council for the Protection of Rural England more congenial and chaired its Amenities Committee for some years.

By this time she was living in a large, detached Victorian house, 'Ravenscroft', in Sutton Road on the outskirts of Shrewsbury. She had also bought a piece of land at Llanymynech, near Oswestry in North Wales, on which she built a small timber bungalow which she always referred to as 'the Shack'. The Shack was her weekend retreat where she could walk the hills she loved and study the plants and the birds. Her *Nature Diaries*, written in a neat, meticulous hand, contain many references to days and weekends spent at Llanymynech, along with tiny detailed drawings of plants and some rather fine colour photographs. Being Hilda, she soon became a committee member of the Llanymynech Rocks Nature Reserve.

In 1970, at the age of sixty-four, she decided to retire and, with no one else in the family willing to continue with the nursery, she sold it to the BBC's popular gardening expert, the late Percy Thrower, who described her as 'one of the world's greatest authorities on old-fashioned and shrub roses'. Still fit and active, she was now to turn her attention to other things.

It is always difficult to paint a true portrait of a person one has never met. Politically she is sometimes described as being 'conservative with a small c', while some of those who knew her insist she was 'apolitical'. Then again it is claimed she was a supporter of the Liberal Party but also of Tories Against Cruise and Trident (TACT). Whatever the truth might be, it is clear from the organisations with which she became involved on her retirement that she was, in the broadest sense, politically involved on many fronts, though never in partisan party-political terms. Only to the paranoid could she have featured as a member of the extreme Left.

She did, however, support the European Nuclear Disarmament movement (END), the Shropshire Anti-Nuclear Alliance, the Shrewsbury Peace Group and the Nuclear Freeze Advertising Campaign. She seems to have become gradually more radical and on at least one occasion she sent money to the Greenham Common women. In 1983 she went so far as to go to London and take part in the massive CND march against Cruise missiles.

She also became involved with ECOROPA, the Welsh-based European Group for Ecological Action, a still somewhat mysterious organisation. ECOROPA was basically an ecological research unit which produced fact sheets on a number of issues from nuclear power to additives in food. It was later to become of compelling interest to the authorities when it deviated from ecology and published an extremely well-informed leaflet *The Falklands War – The Disturbing Truth*. It is written in a question-and-answer format, the answers, it now transpires, having been provided by the man whose name became synonymous with that of the Argentine battleship, *General Belgrano* – Tam Dalyell, ex-Etonian and Labour MP for Linlithgow.

Almost all Hilda's later activity grew out of her lifelong concern for the environment and from 1976 she had been much exercised by the safety aspects of nuclear power. The announcement in 1979 that the then Central Electricity Generating Board (CEGB), ardently backed by the government, was proposing to build the first of a new generation of nuclear power stations at Sizewell in Suffolk concerned her deeply, not least because the new station was to be the first using a pressurised water reactor (PWR), a version of the type of reactor that had recently run amok at Three Mile Island in Pennsylvania and had come within an ace of causing a catastrophic nuclear disaster.

It was some time in 1982 that she made the decision to

become an objector at the forthcoming public inquiry into the building of Sizewell B Nuclear Power Station. Only too aware that the criticisms and concerns of a non-expert would produce the obvious response, Hilda set about considering the most pertinent grounds on which she might object. She read the Department of the Environment's White Paper on *Radioactive Waste Management* (Command No. 8607), described it as 'very disappointing' and decided that it was this issue which might well prove to be the Achilles' heel of the nuclear industry.

As with anything else she had ever undertaken, Hilda set about her task with care and diligence. She needed help from experts – she was, after all, an Arts graduate – and she did not hesitate to turn to them. They included, among others, Sir Kelvin Spencer, who had been a government adviser in the early days of nuclear power but had since changed his mind. He later became chairman of a committee set up under the auspices of the Rowntree Trust to look into the economics of nuclear power and it was his report, *Nuclear Energy – The Real Cost,* published in 1982, which, using the government's own official statistics, put paid once and for all to the argument that nuclear power was cheap. Another expert was Dr Don Arnott, who worked at one time for the International Atomic Energy Agency in Vienna; Hilda also attended a course on nuclear physics at the University of Wales, Aberystwyth.

She seems to have set out on her research with a will, but it is clear that the project did not stop her from enjoying her usual interests, not least the pursuit of rare rock plants. An entry in her *Nature Diaries* in July 1982 shows her bemoaning the traffic caused by holiday-makers, making the place she had stopped for lunch 'intolerable'.

'I left with all speed,' she writes. 'It made departure from Anglesey easier but was an unfortunate note on which to end. Llanberis Pass was the same: every nook that could hold a car had one, and at Penypass they were jam-packed on both sides of the road as well as in the car park. Betws-y-Coed was a seething mass. And August still to come. How long can Wales stand it?'

After her death her many friends remembered a variety of details in attempt to bring her to life. She had a passion for brewing tea in the open air at any time of the day, collecting water from any nearby stream in an old enamel kettle and boiling it up, in early days on an ancient oil heater, then later on a butane gas camping stove. She particularly liked China tea and took it with milk but no sugar: she told a young friend, Catriona Guthrie, that 'sugar made her rheumatism worse'. She dressed in excellent county style and would go miles out of her way to buy a good tweed skirt-length. She enjoyed collecting antique furniture. She had an addiction for 'basking in the sun', when she had the opportunity, sometimes pulling up in the car on long journeys to brew up the inevitable tea and take a nap in a convenient field. She had no fear of travelling and living alone; she enjoyed solitude, 'but was never lonely'.

Charles Sinker says the words and phrases most often used to describe her are 'meticulous', 'a sense of humour' and 'everyone *liked* her'. She is also said to have been 'intelligent', 'charming', 'conscientious', 'nervous of physical violence', 'shy'. She had a ridiculous and enchanting giggle, never knew how to say goodbye on the telephone, showed generosity and friendship, along with 'clarity of thought', 'a sense of purpose', 'indomitable courage' and 'intellectual and moral incorruptibility'. In her late seventies she remained both physically and mentally active and was extremely fit for a woman of her age, apart from some arthritis, which caused her pain, and the migraine headaches with which she had always been cursed.

Sinker says that looking back on the portrait of her that has emerged over the years since her death, he is aware of a totally unbalanced picture of a 'rock-climbing business woman, a rose expert impatient for nature conservation, a thwarted academic obsessed by the threat of nuclear power'.

Her friend Joan Tate, whose husband Clive was a founder member with Hilda of the Shropshire Trust for Nature Conservation, wrote shortly after her death that she took exception to *The Times* obituary suggesting that Hilda was 'eccentric':

'She wasn't. Anyone who veers from what is a very narrow norm can easily be labelled eccentric, but actually Hilda was an extremely conventional person in her ways and not in any way anything like the implication . . . She was very well known indeed, a very independent lady (nothing like that awful photograph except the hat, she always wore them) and also a very private person, very careful with her money, a truthful person in the proper sense. I liked her immensely because of her independence of mind and her persistence in matters in which she thought dishonesty and public lies were involved.'[2]

Throughout 1983 Hilda continued to work diligently at her paper for Sizewell with a view to registering herself officially early in 1984. She decided to call it *An Ordinary Person's View of Radioactive Waste Management.*

The common thread which runs through most people's memories of Hilda is that she was, in Joan Tate's words, 'a very private person'. It is ironic, therefore, that in death she was to become such very public property.

Chapter 2

Death of a Rose-Grower

Sometime over the weekend of the 17/18 March 1984 Hilda was telephoned by a friend, Dr Alicia Symondson. The doctors, John and Alicia Symondson, lived in Kinnersley, not far from Hilda's 'Shack' in Wales. After some general conversation Hilda accepted an invitation to lunch the following Wednesday, 21 March, telling her friend that she expected to arrive about 12.30 p.m.

Perhaps it is as well to mention here two events that are pertinent to what subsequently came to light. On Tuesday 20 March Hilda visited a friend, Constance Purcer, an elderly lady who lived in an isolated house near the village of Aston Munslow, a few miles from Shrewsbury. Miss Purcer was to tell a largely uninterested police force that on that Tuesday afternoon Hilda had wanted to leave 'some papers' with her. Hilda did not seem herself, so much so that at one point Constance describes her as fraught and trembling. Constance, sensing something was far from right, informed Hilda that she preferred not to accept them. Hilda made no attempt to persuade her, merely replacing the papers in a brown envelope which she put in the bottom of her basket under some plants.[1]

Constance assumed the papers must be something to do with

Hilda's work on Sizewell, as Hilda had told her that she had shown them to people in London 'who were very pleased with them'. Hilda also told Constance that she was concerned about the security of her house.

On that same morning, Mrs Mary O'Connor, who lived across the road from Hilda, noticed a young man hanging around on the pavement in front of her house. He had short, curly, blond hair, was clean-shaven, wore jeans and smoked a pipe. Eventually, feeling somewhat uneasy, she went out of her house to have a closer look at him, at which point he quickly crossed the road, jumped over a fence and disappeared. She said that in spite of his clothes he had a military look about him.

While there are chasms of disagreement over the Murrell murder which are unlikely ever to be bridged, there is a fair, if not complete, consensus as to most of the events of the next four days.

Wednesday 21 March
At about 10 a.m. Hilda got into her car, a small white Renault 5, LNT 917W, and drove out of her driveway and into Shrewsbury town centre, where she intended to do some shopping before going on to the Symondsons' for lunch. It is not known whether or not she had originally decided to return home rather than drive straight on to the Symondsons' as her telephone conversation had implied. She drove into the Abbey Foregate area of the town and parked in a side street near Safeways before going into her bank to draw out fifty pounds. She then went into the supermarket and did her shopping, a fact which is confirmed by a friend who saw her there.

At about 10.30 several witnesses remember seeing a red Escort parked in Sutton Road not far from Hilda's house.

At about 11 a.m. it is claimed Hilda made a telephone call, but as this is a matter of controversy, it will be dealt with later.

Between 11.30 and 11.45 a.m. one of Hilda's neighbours, a Mr George Lowe, who had parked his car behind hers near

Safeways, had a brief conversation with her. He remembered that Hilda told him she was not going straight home but in the direction of Monkmoor Road. He saw her set off, then drove away himself to collect mail from his recently sold empty bungalow almost opposite Ravenscroft, after which he drove back along Sutton Road to the fork with the Wenlock Road, opposite St Giles Church. As he was about to pull out to return to the town centre, he saw Hilda waiting to turn right into Sutton Road. Mr Lowe told Hilda's nephew, Robert Green, that obviously Hilda had gone somewhere else, as it was now about fifteen or twenty minutes after he had spoken to her. He also told him that she had seemed quite relaxed and normal. Nothing more is known of where she had been or why.[2]

Hilda drove her car back into her driveway but did not immediately enter her house. First she crossed over the road to Mary O'Connor's house to pay her for a raffle ticket. The ticket cost 15p and Hilda, who did not have the right change, gave Mrs O'Connor 16p. Interestingly, Mrs O'Connor, like Mr Lowe, found nothing odd in Hilda's manner or behaviour. 'She was a very reserved person, a bit old-fashioned perhaps – she always had been and I went to school with her – but on the day she came to see me there was never the slightest suggestion that anything was wrong. I've heard people putting about the idea that she thought someone was after her. It's utter rubbish.' Apart from her murderer and/or his accomplices, no one else ever saw her alive.[3]

Hilda let herself into the house and apparently went upstairs, possibly to change, possibly because she heard something that alarmed her. What one of the participants claims happened next will be dealt with at length later. At this point it is necessary to keep close to the basic facts which came out at the time.

What is clear is that she disturbed an intruder or intruders and, from the injuries she received, appears to have tried to tackle him or them. There was a struggle in a back bedroom where clothes were found on the floor, a struggle which moved out of the room and on to the landing, for one of the vertical railings in the upstairs banister had been knocked out and was later found inside the bathroom door along with the broken-off top piece. The bottom end was still securely attached to the floor.

It is likely that it was during the struggle that Hilda received the severe blow under her right eye (her blind one), which was clearly visible when Robert Green identified her body the following weekend. It was a heavy blow, but he was informed it would not have been sufficient to kill her.

It is now that the story becomes truly bizarre. The obvious reaction of an opportunist thief to the arrival of the owner of a house, especially if it was followed by some kind of an assault, would be to get the hell out of the place as fast as he could. Another might even be that he was so worried that his victim might recognise him that he decided to finish her off there and then. We have become appallingly accustomed in very recent years to tales of thieves beating up and/or killing old people for small sums of money, but ten years ago there were few instances of it. Drugs, the cause of so much of this type of crime, were nothing like such a major problem and crack had not yet put in an appearance.

This thief, however, was special. He did not run away nor make sure his victim was dead. He bundled Hilda, unconscious as she probably was, into her own car and drove off with her. He turned into Sutton Road but did not take the obvious route for a quick getaway. Had he turned away from the direction of the town centre he would have had less than a mile to drive before hitting open country, but he chose instead to turn first towards the town centre, then right again, past the Divisional Headquarters of the West Mercia Police and out into heavy lunchtime traffic. After stopping at traffic lights he turned into Telford Way towards one of many roundabouts, the Heathgate Island, then up Haughmond Hill, and right on to the Hunkington Road.

No fewer than *sixty-nine* witnesses were to come forward and claim they saw Hilda's car being driven fast and erratically along the Newport Road.[4] One is quoted as saying he had to take evasive action to avoid being hit by 'an erratically driven white Renault'. He described the driver as tallish, of medium build and with a narrow, white face and darkish hair. He put his age at about thirty and said the man was wearing a jacket which might have been grey. He also described a woman in the front seat who seemed to be slumped or slouched forward and leaning against the passenger door.

Another witness was a motorcyclist who was one of the people who later agreed to the police taking a statement from him under hypnosis. He says he stopped behind the car at some lights which had been set up because of roadworks. This sighting is given as having taken place just after 1 p.m.

The driver must then have driven the car at top speed out of the town before turning off the main road into Hunkington Lane. The police estimate the journey time from Hilda's house to Hunkington, a distance of six miles which included traffic lights, roundabouts and heavy traffic, as fifteen to twenty minutes in all.

At approximately 1.20 p.m. a local tenant farmer, John Marsh, was driving up Hunkington Lane on his way home for a late lunch when he was surprised to see a small white car slewed into a ditch with its sump stuck on a large stone. Later he was to tell Robert Green that even at that stage he felt somewhat uneasy about it. He carried on home and had his lunch, but the uneasy feeling was reinforced when, on his return to where he was working, he discovered that the car was still there. There was no sign of anyone trying to move it or seeking help to do so. Marsh got out of his own car and walked back to have a look. It appeared to be only superficially damaged and it looked as if an unsuccessful attempt had been made to drive it out of the ditch. Afterwards police said examination showed that it had collided with both sides of the banked verges of the lane before coming to rest.[5]

Marsh tried the door, found it unlocked and looked inside, but saw nothing of any significance. He then returned to work but the abandoned car nagged at the back of his mind until

16

finally he decided to tell the police. He rang his local bobby, Constable Paul Davies, and reported finding a white Renault 5, registration number LNT 917W, abandoned in Hunkington Lane. Davies took down the details and duly reported the matter to his superiors in Shrewsbury.

Shortly after 2 p.m. a number of people reported seeing the person who became known as 'the running man'. He was seen 'jogging' from the Hunkington area about lunchtime and again between 2 p.m. and 2.30 p.m. in Sundorne Road, a road which turns off the Heathgate Island roundabout. Later the police, in spite of their belief in the opportunist burglar, reconstructed a route for him back into Shrewsbury which retraced the journey made by Hilda's car. The running man was described by witnesses as being between the ages of twenty-five and forty, five foot six to seven inches tall, slim and with fair hair. He wore a grey jacket and his trouser bottoms and trainers were wet and muddy as though he had run across fields. He was sighted also in Telford Way, where police consider he might have hitched a lift. In all, twelve witnesses saw and described what certainly appears to be the same running man.

When Hilda did not arrive at the Symondsons' home as expected, they were obviously a little alarmed. Alicia Symondson could not understand why Hilda, always so meticulous about such matters, had not telephoned either to say she could be delayed or that she had been prevented from coming altogether. Sometime after one, therefore, Alicia rang Hilda. The phone rang out normally but as there was no reply, she assumed that Hilda must have been delayed but was now on her way over. Later, when there was still no sign of Hilda, she rang Ravenscroft a second time. Again the telephone rang out and again there was no reply. Alicia could not understand it.

Thursday 22 March
Throughout Thursday Hilda's car remained in the ditch. The police were to give a conflicting series of responses as to why nothing was done about it. Early that morning, one of Hilda's

neighbours, a Mrs Reekie, noted that the curtains were still drawn in Hilda's house and the lights on.[6]

At three o'clock that afternoon a Mr Ian Scott visited the Moat, a copse at the top of the hill above where the car had been seen. His wife owned the land farmed by John Marsh and he had gone to the copse to examine trees. He was trying to decide if any should be felled and, if so, which these might be. In so doing he covered every bit of the copse as he counted the trees to establish what was the best course to pursue. It was too early in the year for there to be much undergrowth.

Early in the investigation he told the police and others that there was no body in the Moat that Thursday afternoon and that there could not have been, as 'I examined the place so thoroughly I would have seen if there'd been a dead rabbit there, let alone a person'. He has stuck by his testimony but has subsequently refused to discuss the matter any further, intensely disliking the suggestion that there might be a political dimension to the story.[7]

Later the same day a tractor-driver working in a nearby field saw a large, dark car drive up Hunkington Lane. It parked in the gateway to a field, opposite where Hilda's glasses, hat and a knife were later found. A man was seen to leave the car and walk over to the Moat, where he remained for about twenty minutes before returning to the car and driving away. Car and driver have never been traced. It was not Ian Scott.[8]

Friday 23 March
During Friday friends and relatives telephoned Hilda at Ravenscroft without success. All heard the telephone ring out. Some also tried the Shack at Llanymynech and were equally disappointed as the line appeared to be out of order all together.

At 9 a.m. Brian George, who undertook gardening work for Hilda, passed Ravenscroft and saw the curtains drawn and the lights still on. He looked across to the house and noticed that the kitchen door was ajar, but as he was not due to work there that day he did not investigate further, assuming that Hilda was getting on with some housework and had left the door open but had not yet bothered to open the curtains.[9]

At 10.30 a.m. John Marsh returned to Hunkington Lane to see if the white car was still there. When he found that it was, he once again rang PC Davies and asked him if he had done anything about it. Davies confirmed that he had reported the car to Shrewsbury Police immediately after Marsh had contacted him the first time.[10]

That afternoon, according to the police, a red Escort was seen driving slowly past the field, known as 'the Funeral Field', which lies between the Moat and Hunkington Lane. The grisly name has nothing to do with any earlier murder but was given to that piece of ground because its heavy, marshy soil made it hard work for horses in the days of ploughing which, therefore, was done at a funereal pace. The red Escort was seen again three times in the course of the next hour and a half.

Early in the evening the police finally followed up the abandoned Renault 5 and discovered its ownership. They found nothing 'sinister' about it, they said, but a police constable was sent round to Ravenscroft to tell Hilda.[11] In a later statement he said, 'I found signs of habitation and the back door was unlocked, but I did not search the house as nothing seemed amiss.' There was no mention of the kitchen door being found ajar or of curtains drawn and lights left on.

At 6.30 p.m. a man claims he was visited by the Shrewsbury Police. He has understandably wanted to remain anonymous, as he works both in education and as a professional counsellor to people with sexual problems, often of a severe nature. He told both myself and Tam Dalyell, at the House of Commons in January of the next year, that the police asked if he was 'all right'. He presumed this was a reference to an event during which one of the people he had been counselling had become violent, but he was surprised the police were still following the matter up. He replied that of course he was.

The police then asked if he could think of anybody who might have a sexual hang-up about elderly ladies. Did he know of someone who would be turned on by going into a woman's bedroom and interfering with her clothing? Someone who might be violent? After some discussion the police went away, leaving the man wondering what on earth it had all been about. He says, 'I realised when I read the first reports in the paper the next evening of the finding of Hilda Murrell's body that it seemed the police had been describing the murder, but I'm at a loss to understand why they came to me on the Friday night when she wasn't found until the Saturday.'[12]

Much later that night a witness who lives near the Moat claims she saw 'lights and movement' in the copse.

Saturday 24 March
At 6.30 a.m. the constable who had called round the previous evening returned to Ravenscroft. There are discrepancies in the reports of how the police constable got into the house as the local media quote West Mercia Police as saying he broke in, while Robert Green says the constable found the key in the back door and let himself in; he later left the key with a relative, Frances Murrell. Hilda, as we shall see later, had complained some weeks previously that her spare key, kept hanging on a hook outside, had gone missing.

Just after 8.30 a.m. Brian George arrived to work on the garden as usual and met a 'bearded policeman' about to leave. Here the first element of black farce creeps into the story, for the policeman told George he had spent two hours inside Ravenscroft and looked around the house 'pretty thoroughly', although he had not gone into Hilda's bedroom as 'he did not want to disturb the old lady'. He added, however, that 'he did think the old lady was a bit untidy'. He had looked around the rest of the house from attic to cellar and left the lights on as he had found them. Having imparted this information he left. Brian George says, 'He was in the house for two hours and hadn't noticed Hilda Murrell wasn't there!'[13]

At about 9 a.m. a second gardener, David Williams, arrived

and the two men began to set out their tools and plan their morning's work, both remarking that it was odd they had not seen Hilda around for a few days. After some further discussion they decided that in spite of the visit from the policeman they would see for themselves if Hilda was all right. Whatever the truth about the key to the kitchen door, the two men were able to get into the house through the conservatory.

Although the police were to backtrack on it later there is no doubt that at first they told the local media that the house was 'ransacked'.[14] This was never true and Williams and George would certainly have been aware of it had it been the case. There was, however, such clear evidence of a break-in that the two men could not credit the fact that the police constable had told George he had found nothing suspicious. 'Any layman would recognise instantly that there was something wrong,' said Mr George. 'There was washing on the floor and seed packets around the place. We found a couple of handbags and general mail on the table in the scullery.'

The two men called up the stairs just in case Hilda was there all the time but received no reply; they thought that possibly she had decided, without telling anyone, to spend a few days at the Shack. It was when they attempted to telephone Llanymynech to find out and, if she was indeed there, to inform her of the break-in, that they discovered the telephone at Ravenscroft was not working.

They immediately went to Brian George's house and rang from there. They were answered by the whining noise which shows a phone is out of order. By now thoroughly alarmed, the men returned to Ravenscroft, bringing with them Hilda's cleaning lady, Betty Latter. This time they made a more thorough search and discovered three days' newspapers and mail lying behind the front door where they had fallen. They returned at once to George's house and telephoned the police. After doing so they realised they had given them the wrong street number for Ravenscroft, 52 instead of 72. After a few minutes they went round to 52 and found a policewoman standing outside. All three returned to Ravenscroft where they were joined shortly afterwards by the bearded policeman George had spoken to earlier that morning.

The five people remained in the house until a Superintendent Needham of Shrewsbury Police arrived. Confirming that the telephone did not work, he asked George if he might use his home phone and when George asked why he did not use the radiophone in the police car, Needham insisted he use George's, saying that he had to make a 'private call'. He then left for George's house. It was about 10.30 a.m.[15]

At about 10.15 a.m. Robert Green had received a telephone call from his cousin Stella, who lived in Shrewsbury and who told him that another relative had just rung her to say that Hilda appeared to be missing and so did her car. Robert Green then rang Shrewsbury Police but could discover nothing.

Meanwhile there had been activity outside Shrewsbury. Sometime after 10 a.m., the same PC Paul Davies who had twice reported Hilda's abandoned car called at the home of a local gamekeeper to ask if he would help search the surrounding area for a missing person. The man was out, but his wife, Mrs Chris Randall, was at home and immediately agreed to help. She gave the policeman a lift in her van, taking her two Labrador dogs with them.

They parked near the abandoned Renault and walked over to the Moat, which was the only area in the immediate vicinity in which anything might reasonably have been concealed. Mrs Randall's dogs found Hilda's body almost straight away. It was lying in a slight depression in the ground. The time was just on 10.30 a.m.

The body was face up and Mrs Randall noted that the knees were scratched and bloody. It was clothed in a brown coat and a pullover, but was naked from the waist down. The skirt was lying nearby. Hilda's car keys were found in the pocket of her coat. She had been stabbed a number of times.

The weapon identified, an eight-inch cook's knife from her own kitchen, was found in the hedge near the road, along with her driving glasses and floppy hat. Her rubber overshoes were found in the field in front of the copse where her body was discovered.

The 'private call' made by Superintendent Needham was to Chief Superintendent David Cole, the head of West Mercia CID. He had earned himself a certain amount of publicity on two previous occasions. The first had been some years earlier when he was the number two on what became known as the 'Black Panther' case. His superior had become very emotionally involved in the disappearance of the victim, Leslie Whittle, and earned a reputation for promising that an arrest was imminent. Leslie Whittle's body was eventually found in an underground bunker. She had died of 'vagal inhibition' – fright. Cole himself had led the inquiry the previous year into the Geoffrey Prime scandal at General Communications Headquarters, GCHQ, Cheltenham. Prime, at one time a neo-Nazi, had openly bragged that he was spying for months before he was finally arrested.

Having spoken to Cole, Needham returned to Ravenscroft where he told the waiting group that Cole had informed him that the body of a woman had been found and was thought to be that of Hilda Murrell.

Just before midday Robert Green was contacted and asked if he would come to Shrewsbury to identify his aunt.

Chapter 3

'We'll Catch the Killer . . .'

The story broke first in the *Shropshire Star*, which was to give extensive coverage to the ensuing investigation for many months. Under the headline 'Rose Expert Is Murdered!', there followed a description of the finding of the body, with pictures of the number plate of Hilda's car, police at work and a photograph of Hilda wearing the usual floppy hat.

Details of the report of the Home Office pathologist who carried out the first post mortem were not released for a further eight months but need to be noted now, not least because there is still controversy over how exactly Hilda died.

The pathologist, Dr Peter Acland, described first how he had accompanied police to a small copse at 11.30 a.m. on the morning of 24 March.[1] The body was wearing a buttoned–up brown overcoat and two jumpers, he said, and was naked from the waist down, apart from a sock. The second sock was found with the skirt nearby.

The body was cold to the touch and rigor mortis was beginning to wear off. 'There was bruising and blood around the left side of the face. There were cuts to the palms of both hands. Both knees were severely abraded and there was pink discolouration. There was a bruise on the left hip. On pulling up the clothing, several wounds were noticed in the right upper abdomen. . . There was no obvious evidence of bruising or injury to the neck. There was no evidence of petechial haemorrhages in the eyes. There was some bloodstaining on opening the coat from the region of the abdomen. Car keys and a bloodstained handkerchief were found in the right coat pocket. There was slight bruising and swelling to the left wrist – evidence of rheumatoid arthritis. . . There had been heavy rain within the previous twenty-four hours but earlier that week it had been very cold and dry.'

Dr Acland carried out the post mortem that evening. Hilda's general state of health, apart from the arthritis, had been very good. Rigor was now rapidly wearing off and the first important point he noted, again, were the large areas of abrasion on both her knees. There were no scalp injuries but 'on the right side of the face was a diffuse bruise, over the right forehead, around the right eye, acrosss the right cheek, measuring ten by six centimetres. There was a split in the skin just below the right eye. The nature of this injury was probably due to a broad blunt impact. This could be due to the car accident, but equally likely due to kicking. It is slightly less likely to be due to punching, although this is still a possibility.' This was the bruise noted by Robert Green.

There was a small bruise to the left side of the chin which could be due to punching or falling, two faint scratches to the left side of the neck and a small bruise to the mid-lower neck. Some dried blood was present in the right ear. 'She had a cataract in her right eye.' (This is the eye in which Hilda had been blind from infancy.) The mouth appeared uninjured. There was a large bruise over the right shoulder and upper portion of the chest, corresponding to the fracture of the collar bone and, on the right arm, twelve centimetres below the point of the shoulder, an incised wound corresponding to a smaller one on the other side of the arm. 'A probe showed communication between the two wounds, and hence a penetrating wound had transfixed the arm at this point.' There was a superficial scratch running down from chest to abdomen and a group of penetrating incised wounds, as already noted, on the right upper abdomen. Two of these were sufficiently deep to have damaged the liver. The autopsy showed a little loose blood in the abdominal cavity.

'In my opinion,' said Dr Acland, 'the wounds were disabling but not fatal.'

He noted again the scratches and abrasion on the knees, a laceration on the ankle and that 'there was no evidence macroscopically of sexual assault'. In view of subsequent press releases by the police that needs to be noted. There were a number of injuries to the hands – an abrasion at the base of the right thumb, a cut across it, a further cut extending across the palm of the hand and a bruise on the wrist. The cut across the hand was 'consistent with a defensive wound, as though grasping at a sharp implement'. There was bruising over the knuckles of the left hand and small cuts on the palm, again consistent with defensive wounds.

All Hilda's major organs were normal, apart from the liver wounds, and the stomach contained the remains of some coffee. 'Numerous punctate erosions were noted in the mucosa which is a feature consistent with hypothermia.' Summarising again the wounds to the body Acland concluded, 'I don't think she died of blood loss.' Regarding the superficial wounds to the hands he repeated that he thought these were defensive. 'They are typical injuries you would see in somebody who is fighting off an attack from a sharp weapon. I think the weapon was probably a knife. I can't confidently say whether it was a single- or double-bladed knife, but probably more likely to be a single-bladed knife.

'It is possible that had she received medical treatment immediately after the attack, she would not have died. I think that an elderly lady with some moderately serious injuries in very cold weather would die of hypothermia within five to ten hours. Had she received medical treatment within that period she may have survived.'

Acland then entered the realm of speculation. Miss Murrell,

26

he said, might have been trying to escape from the car and been pursued and possibly frog-marched with an arm across her neck, and the knife held towards her. 'The abrasions to her knees were consistent with her crawling. This may explain, in fact, why some of her lower clothing may have come away from her as she was crawling along on her knees . . .'

Having enlarged on this he added, 'I wouldn't like to say whether the abrasions on the hands were consistent with crawling or whether they were due to the assault. The abrasions on the knees could have been consistent with her being dragged. This is a possibility, but I did not notice any other abrasions to the wrists, legs or to the toes which you might expect if she was dragged. I can't exclude she might have been dragged.' Later Dr Acland would reiterate that he believed the cause of death to be hypothermia. He also told a journalist that he remained firmly of the opinion that the body had not been moved after death, although hypothetically, if two people had been involved in lifting her, it was possible.

Dr Acland's evidence will be returned to later but suffice it to say that there are a number of experts, including pathologists, who say that it is almost impossible to determine whether hypothermia was the cause of death when a body has lain out in the open for several days. A woman pathologist also told me she would like to try, with a living woman, to see if it were possible for her knickers and skirt to fall off merely because she was crawling around. As to moving a body after death, the usual way of discovering whether this has occurred is by examining the phenomenon known as hypostasis or post mortem lividity. Hypostasis is the draining of the blood to the lowest area of the body when circulation stops. Within six to eight hours the resulting purple stains are fixed. Patches of white skin are, however, left where the body has been in contact with the surface on which it lies and, because of this, it is usually apparent if a body has been moved after lying for some time in one position.

One thing seems certain, however: Hilda fought for her life.

When the police searched Hilda's house after the finding of her body, they did note – this time – that the curtains had been closed and the lights left on.[2] There was also a pool of water by the back door, a damp rolled-up sheet found downstairs, the signs of struggle in the bedroom and several handbags standing open on a table. The media reports of the first day of investigation all have the police describing Ravenscroft as having been 'ransacked'. The scene-of-crime video, however, shows drawers and cupboards opened but a generally tidy interior to the lounge and living room. Indeed, it appears that, far from ransacking the place, the intruder or intruders had systematically gone through everything, including Hilda's papers and books, which had then been replaced in their original positions; this latter point was emphasised by Chief Superintendent Cole at the inquest in spite of his faith in the theory that Hilda had interrupted an opportunist burglar. In answer to criticism on this point, West Mercia Police later denied they had ever suggested that the house had been ransacked.[3]

The same edition of the *Shropshire Star* notes the 'Riddle of Car Found in Beauty Spot Ditch'[4], commenting that 'local people did not pay very much attention to the car. Cars in ditches are a familiar sight in that area and it was only later police were called. At least two people claim that, early in the investigation, when they asked police why the report of the abandoned car had not been followed up, they were told that it had, but that the wrong number had been fed into the Swansea computer, one that had led them to pursue inquiries in Scotland. This was later denied.

When I asked the Shrewsbury Police some time after Hilda's death why the first sighting of the car had not been checked out I was told, 'The white Renault car was first seen in the ditch on March 21st by a member of the public who notified the local police. There appeared to be no superficial damage.

As there appeared to be nothing wrong with the car and it was not causing an obstruction no further action was taken at the time.'

In response to my asking why not, in view of the fact that the car was not very old and might have been a stolen one which had already been reported and for which they were looking, I was told, 'Vehicles are abandoned in similar circumstances all over the country. Some 2,000 such incidents occur in F division of Shrewsbury annually. It would be impossible to completely investigate every such incident.' It should be pointed out here that car theft had not reached such epidemic proportions in 1984 as it has now.

Wednesday the 28th dawned with the headline 'Police Fear Cover Up'. This was not prophetic of what was to come but suggested 'someone may be shielding the brutal killer of Hilda Murrell. Police say the murderer may have been bloodstained, that he may be a local man and that someone may be withholding information.' Chief Superintendent Cole released the news that several witnesses had come forward to say they had seen a small white car being driven erratically along Telford Way and that they were fairly certain the driver was a man. Also that a knife, possibly used during the attack, had been found in a hedge, along with Hilda's hat and glasses.

Cole admitted that the 'circumstances of the murder are very unusual' and added, 'It is proving a difficult inquiry.' Witnesses who may have seen 'a running man', a description of whom had been issued the previous day, were asked to come forward.

Those who turned to the *Star* the next day, Thursday 29 March, might have been forgiven for thinking the murderer was as good as caught. 'Police Net Closing In . . .' was the headline, while, according to the intro, 'The net is tightening around the brutal killer of Hilda Murrell. Police say they are close and that they need just one vital breakthrough. They believe the public hold the key. That is the dramatic news today from the man leading sixty police officers in the hunt for one of Shropshire's most savage murderers.'

It was at this point that Cole revealed that the telephone wires in Hilda's house had been 'torn out'. This piece of information is incorrect and is so crucial it will be returned to later.

This was followed by a further appeal for witnesses and a repeat of information already given, but, to be fair to the police, nothing in their press release really merits so confident a headline. Indeed, Cole says, 'We may still be in a position where someone knows the assailant or can point a finger at him, but for reasons best known to them have not yet come forward. We would appeal to their better nature to come forward.' There was always a possibility that the killer could strike again if interrupted during the course of a burglary. However, he added that inquiries so far had not been able to establish whether or not anything had actually been stolen from the house: indeed, it looked as if nothing had been taken.

By the next day, 30 March, this view had altered with the news that fifty pounds had been stolen, the amount Hilda had drawn out of her bank on the day she was killed. The photograph accompanying this piece of information shows two 'forensic officers in space-age scene-of-crime suits carefully checking every item inside Miss Murrell's home'.

That was also the day when the inquest into her death was opened. Police Constable Cedric Harold McCormick of the West Mercia Constabulary swore on oath in Shrewsbury Magistrates' Court that 'At 6.15 p.m. on Saturday 24 March 1984 I attended the mortuary of the Royal Shrewsbury Hospital and there met Mr Graham Hartley Davies, a Company Director of Pontesford House, Pontesford, Shropshire. At the mortuary he was shown the body of a female which he identified as being that of Hilda Murrell. She was born February 1906 at Shrewsbury and was a spinster.' The coroner then adjourned the inquest until 25 July. In the event it did not take place until the following December.

On Saturday came the first whiff of one of the two strands which were to haunt the Murrell case, the nuclear connection.[5] In a down-page item, 'Murder Victim Left an Unfinished

Report', it was noted that Hilda had been working on a paper on the subject of nuclear waste which she was to present to the Sizewell Public Inquiry. Her friend Mrs Diana Moss is quoted as saying that it was hoped by her friends that her paper could be presented posthumously.

The bigger headline, however, was 'Hunt on for the Running Man'[6], as the police now believed that the man who had driven Hilda along Telford Way fitted the description of the man seen running from Hunkington back towards Shrewsbury on the day of the murder. A Superintendent Mayne said they were anxious that the man should come forward as, if he was an innocent party, he could be eliminated from the inquiries. The report continues: 'He [Mayne] said the major differences between his description and that of the killer were probably explained by the fact that people had only "fleeting glances" at the man who drove Miss Murrell's car from her home in Sutton Road.' It was also revealed that there had been 'a further tragedy' during the course of the investigation. A man being interviewed as part of the routine inquiry had collapsed and died, it was believed as the result of a heart attack.

On 7 April police published an artist's impression of the running man and two policemen ran the route it was thought he had taken to try and jog memories.[7] This artist's impression has been the object of hilarity over the years since a second one, issued in the July, looks as unlike the first as might possibly be imagined. Only now, with hindsight, does it seem as if the first picture might well have been an accurate one of the man seen near Hunkington.

By Monday 9 April police were desperately trying any leads, including asking any charity collectors, who might have been calling in Sutton Road on the day of the murder, to contact them. On 13 April the *Star* told its readers that a new rose was to be named after Hilda by famous rose-grower David Austin, and that it would be launched at the Chelsea Flower Show. In the event this did not happen as the rose simply refused to flower.

On 11 April Cole admitted that the inquiry was a very difficult one. A good deal of information which had come in was still being sifted and 'I am confident, given the support of the public, that we can bring this matter to a successful conclusion. The inquiry is in its third week, so it is still in its early stages. It is not uncommon for murder inquiries to stretch for more than three months. There comes a time of evaluation in any criminal inquiry when all the information has to be analysed. That doesn't necessarily mean the trail goes cold – far from it. We have reached that stage of evaluation now but are still going forward.' More than eighty officers were still working on the case. The police theory was then restated – that Miss Murrell had disturbed a robber on returning home, had been bundled into her car, driven away and left to die. The headline? 'We'll Catch the Killer – Police Chief.'

On 18 April there was a down-page story in the *Star* which one might have expected to have been the front-page lead. Two petty thieves had come up before Shrewsbury Magistrates charged with stealing a tax disc from Hilda's car on the day she was murdered. When they learned who it belonged to they had panicked and burnt the disc, the court was told. Charles Ronald Bevan (21) and Christopher Raymond Watton (18) admitted stealing the vehicle licence and Watton also admitted driving a car which was uninsured and without an MOT and that he had failed to produce his driving licence. Bevan was given a twelve-month conditional discharge, while Watton's case was adjourned for reports as to whether or not he would be suitable for community service.

'You can imagine,' said the defendant's solicitor, 'the fright these two young men had when they discovered why the car was in the area.' To this day there has never been any explanation as to why nothing was made of this astonishing piece of information nor whether the police had discovered anything of use to them from the young men concerned who, after all, had actually been inside the car on the day Hilda died. It was left to a television programme to interview the two young men and get their story.

The sensational news, it seems, was kept for the following day, 19 April. The *Star* headlined 'Sex Attack on Murdered Woman – Police.' 'Murdered Hilda Murrell was the victim of a sex attack, police have revealed today. Forensic tests have established that she was sexually assaulted at her home in Sutton Road, Shrewsbury, before being driven to her death six miles away in a wood near Haughmond Hill. "But there was no evidence of rape," said Detective Chief Superintendent David Cole of West Mercia CID. "This is a particularly disgusting thing, an assault of this nature on a seventy-eight-year-old perfectly respectable woman. The sexual motive opens many more avenues of inquiry."'

It should be remembered that the post mortem carried out on the day Hilda was found, details of which should have been in police hands by the next day, specifically stated that there was no evidence of any sexual assault.

Also, for the first time, the police asked for information regarding two cars, a red Ford Escort seen in Sutton Road at around at 10.30 a.m. on the day of the murder and a 'large dark car seen at 4 p.m. in Hunkington Lane, parked in the gateway to a field opposite where Miss Murrell's spectacles and hat, along with a knife thought to be "the murder weapon" were found'.

The question of the sexual assault has been a matter of bitter controversy. At no time did Cole say that Hilda had been raped, although some reports assumed this to be the case, but police follow-ups to the original press statement are, to say the least, confusing. Depending on which police spokesman they approached, reporters were offered conflicting statements: that there had been an actual sexual assault; that there was evidence of masturbatory activity; that traces of semen had been found on clothing but that these were too faint to be of use; and that the traces of semen were strong enough to show that the person had had a vasectomy. Police later agreed that while some details

33

had been withheld to prevent distress to the family and 'for operational reasons', 'some confusion has occurred over two police press releases'.[8]

On the same day a memorial service was held for Hilda in St Chad's Church, Shrewsbury. On the altar was a single vase of roses. The Bishop of Shrewsbury, the Right Reverend Leslie Rees, spoke of the sense of outrage and shock at Hilda's murder: 'We all feel caught up in it and diminished by it and yet, in a strange way, we are brought close to one another in our revulsion and in our sorrow.' He described Hilda as 'an elusive but remarkable person, a private person who chose to reveal only a part of herself to each friend'.

April ended with no more confident headlines. No new information had come in on either the red Escort or the dark saloon car. West Mercia Police confirmed press reports that they had brought in a hypnotist to question key witnesses.

From the media reports and police statements it would be impossible to guess that underneath the official story of the police investigation there ran an unofficial sub-text, a sub-text which would eventually surface and blow the story of the murder of a Shropshire rose-grower into a full-scale political *cause célèbre*.

Chapter 4

Fearful for her Life

At first Hilda's friends were too stunned and horrified at her violent death to think of anything else. As time went on, however, recollections of Hilda's last few weeks began to surface, along with a feeling of dissatisfaction over the progress of the police investigation.

As the Bishop of Shrewsbury had said, Hilda was a person who revealed only a part of herself to each friend. It is not surprising, therefore, that it took some time for the parts to come together.

The frequency of entries in Hilda's *Nature Diaries* falls off in the last two years of her life and this might well be due to the amount of time and effort she was putting into her paper for Sizewell. The last entries were made in the summer and the September of 1983 and tell of her continued search for rare plants. On 22 June she went to Anglesey and found ten flowers of the Fragrant Orchid in a marshy place the whereabouts of which she did not want to reveal. She notes that her 'Joe Brown boots still don't let in a drop'. After a large lunch eaten at the roadside, she visited an exhibition of Moslem crafts at a weavers' gallery where she drank a 'huge cup of tea', having been unable to find a suitable stream to allow her to brew up in the open.

The last entry of all, on 26 September, describes how she looked out across the hills from Llanymynech very early in the morning, their tops showing above bands of low-lying white fog. But the 'really wonderful sight' was not this but a maze of cobwebs: '. . . not the usual kind but three-dimensional ones, nearer fabric than thread, so close-woven was the gossamer. The dew had been heavy and they were spangled with droplets so small that I counted twenty of them on a bare inch of thread, but though minute they were brilliant reflectors of pure celestial light. Miraculously, I had the sun behind me when I bent to look at one of them, to find an inverted rainbow lying across it, very softly orange and green and blue, living specks of opal. The fineness of the filigree was breathtaking.'

A more serene picture can hardly be imagined. Yet within six months Hilda was dead and before that she had not been herself. She, so independent and quick to rubbish foolish fancies, was beginning to show signs of what might unkindly be described as paranoia. She spoke of surveillance, suggested that her telephone might be tapped, her mail intercepted. Speaking as someone who suffered exactly the same problems when I first began investigating the Murrell murder, I can only say that one is very chary of mentioning such suspicions even to close friends for fear of being thought to be suffering from delusions.

Even people who were extremely sympathetic to what she was doing considered that her views, while researching the nuclear industry, had become somewhat eccentric. She had come to believe in what she described as a 'nuclear Bruderbond', a fellowship between international nuclear scientists which transcended all political boundaries.[1]

This may be rather far-fetched, but there is some proof of at least sympathy among international nuclear enthusiasts. An example of this is the reaction of British nuclear scientists to the revelation by the dissident Russian scientist, Dr Zhores Medvedev, after his defection to the West, that there had been a catastrophic explosion of nuclear waste at Kyshtym near Chelyabinsk in the Urals in 1957. He had assumed that

36

it was known in the West through intelligence sources, even though the Soviet nuclear establishment had always denied it, and so he was totally unprepared for the reaction caused by his description of the event when he wrote about it in the *New Scientist* in November 1976. Afterwards he said:

'I was unaware at that time that this nuclear disaster was absolutely unknown to Western experts and my article created an unexpected sensation. Reports about this twenty-year-old nuclear disaster appeared in almost all the major newspapers. At the same time, some Western nuclear experts, including the chairman of the UK Atomic Energy Authority, Sir John Hill, tried to dismiss my story as "science fiction", "rubbish", or "a figment of my imagination". Such an accident, said Hill, "was impossible". Later it was coyly admitted that the incident had been known by the CIA all along and that they had passed the relevant information on to Britain.'[2] British and American nuclear experts also hung on in with their Russian counterparts in playing down the hazards of the Chernobyl disaster in 1986 during the early days. So Hilda was not completely over the top in her belief in a 'Bruderbond', even if it is neither as organised nor as sinister as she imagined.

It was in the early part of 1984 that Hilda's fears surfaced to the point that they really concerned her friends. On 18 February she attended a meeting held in Shrewsbury by the Medical Campaign Against Nuclear Weapons, one of the organisers of which was Dr Harry Bury. He had invited her along because he thought, in view of her Sizewell paper, that she would be interested to learn how civilian plutonium can be converted for military use. Dr Bury describes her at the time as being 'frightened of late and very secretive'.

On 25 February Gerard Morgan-Grenville of ECOROPA received a strange phone call from Hilda, a call confirmed by his wife Fern, who had to carry messages back and forth to begin with as he was in the bath. 'Hilda did sound very worried when I answered the phone,' she said. 'I can't think why, I can't put my finger on it exactly; but whatever it was it made me call my husband from the bathroom. There was no question of saying "He'll call you back" – she did sound uncharacteristically upset.'[3] Hilda's manner must have been odd, as Morgan-Grenville, who would have experienced her apparent inability to conclude telephone conversations, was prepared to sit shivering in a bathrobe in a cold corridor to take the call.

Although Hilda sounded anxious the conversation was discursive. She brought up points from her Sizewell paper and mused on at length about how long the Conservative government was likely to last, while the unfortunate Morgan-Grenville dripped and froze. All in all she remained on the telephone for half an hour, by which time he describes himself as being 'frozen stiff'. It was, however, her parting words as she finally rang off that remained in the minds of the Morgan-Grenvilles long after: 'If they don't get me first, I want the world to know that one old woman has seen through their lies.' They had no idea what she meant.

On 12 March Ian and Thalia Campbell attended a European election meeting in Llangollen, after which they spent the night at the home of a friend. She told them that Hilda Murrell (whom they knew) had expressed concern for her own safety, and before the Campbells left for home the following morning another of Hilda's acquaintances came round and reinforced the point.[4]

Hilda is said to have registered herself officially as an individual objector at the Sizewell public inquiry in mid-March, following a discussion with Peter Bunyard of *The Ecologist* magazine to whom she sometimes turned for information. He advised her that she would have to make her formal application in writing and that she would also be asked to supply, at the very least, a detailed synopsis of what she was going to say.

She spent the weekend of 18/19 March at Llanymynech and on the Monday morning called in and had breakfast with a friend whom she told she had finally completed her Sizewell paper. Presumably she meant that she had finalised her draft, as the day before she died she noted in her personal diary that she had 'started altering the draft'. It was that afternoon that she called in on Constance Purcer, asking if she could leave the papers and mentioning her concern about security. According to Robert Green she was worried because the spare key which always hung in a relatively hidden position outside the house seemed to have disappeared.

Constance Purcer told the police about Hilda's papers in April when, at her insistence, they visited her for a second time, but the information she gave them was not made public. It is therefore unlikely that it could have been known to Laurens Otter.

Laurens Otter alleges that Hilda rang him sometime between 11 and 11.30 a.m. on the day of her abduction. The point that needs emphasising here is that the police have never taken him, in my opinion at least, seriously enough, not least because he did not surface with his information until months after the murder. Otter's story is that he wrote to me at least twice when he knew I was looking into the Murrell business. This might well be true, as at that time half my mail was either going astray or arriving very obviously having been tampered with. Otter chose to contact me because years before, when I was the West of England correspondent for the *Guardian*, he had been a copytaker; I had every reason to remember him, for he was extraordinarily pedantic and I have the strongest recollections of standing in telephone boxes as the deadline drew ever nearer on a news story, trying to dictate it down the line to a man who would pick me up for repeating adjectives or suggest I rephrased the last sentence. The consequent heated altercations were recollected by both of us.

Otter states that Hilda, whom he had met only rarely at meetings of the Shropshire Peace Alliance, rang him from what was obviously a public call box, explained who she was, then asked if he could possibly come over to Shrewsbury to pick up and look after some papers for her. Otter lives in Wellington and explained that this would be difficult as he had no car as his wife used it for going to work – she is a teacher. They then discussed the possibility of trains and Otter consulted a local railway timetable. The first train he could catch would not have got him into Shrewsbury until about 1 p.m. and Hilda said this would be too late as she was going to visit friends for lunch. The request to deposit papers certainly echoes Constance Purcer's story. However, Otter also alleges that Hilda told him she felt she was under some kind of surveillance and that she was expecting a visit from an Inspector Davies or Davy. She did not know what it was about. The call ended with her suggesting that she might bring the papers along to that evening's meeting of the Shropshire Peace Alliance if she was back from Wales in time. When she did not turn up he naturally assumed she had got back too late to do so. No one else ever heard Hilda refer to a proposed visit by a police inspector.

Otter's acquaintances and indeed Otter himself put the failure of the police to follow up his information down to the fact that he had a past history of political direct action, was a well-known peace activist and 'agitator' and was associated with a number of Left-orientated groups. Otter also thinks that it was because Hilda knew this too that she decided he was an ideal candidate to hide her papers. The police may have felt that Otter, a known troublemaker, might have invented the story to cash in on the Murrell murder. The truth, so long after the event, is unlikely ever to be known.[5]

Hilda's friend, Joan Tate, summed up the reaction, at the end of the first weeks of the investigation, of those in Hilda's circle who had been only too keen to assist: 'General impressions have been that; a) some of the police did not even know who Hilda was; b) did not even know how to pronounce her name (although she and her family firm were immensely well known around here); c) what is told to the public via newspapers is not always in keeping with what some of the public know; and d) the police are not very good at handling all the more articulate members of the public.'

The young policeman who took her own statement wrote down that Hilda was always 'kurtius'. 'Not that spelling matters all that much,' said Joan Tate, 'but if they had had tape recorders then perhaps what one actually said could have been transferred to someone who understood from listening.' Her statement, she continued, 'bore very little relation to what I actually said'.[6] One witness was described as 'unreliable' because although she was a 'highly respectable lady' she was also a member of CND. Mrs Tate described herself as being disappointed in the police whom she had hitherto considered to be fair, sensible and interested in the common good. 'A number of people who have come forward rather diffidently with bits of information – as we were all urged to do, it's called the co-operation of the public – have been treated extremely offensively and made to seem foolish. Not the best way to guarantee public co-operation in the future, I think.'

The police interviewed Constance Purcer very shortly after the murder, when she was still in a state of shock. Afterwards she realised that she had not told them about Hilda wanting to leave her papers with her and, thinking this might in some way be relevant, contacted the special incident room which had been set up in Shrewsbury Police headquarters and asked if she could talk to a senior officer, preferrably an inspector. Remarkably enough, at a time when the police were daily asking through the media for anyone who thought they might have further information to come forward, they did not appear to be interested, even when Robert Green asked them on her behalf. Finally, Constance became so determined that she rang again and again until it was agreed someone would be sent out to see her.

On 16 April, when the story was still taking up acres of the *Shropshire Star*, two young detectives arrived. After complaining that she had specifically asked to speak to a senior officer, she tried to tell them about Hilda and the papers. Their response was to demand if either Robert Green or anyone from Harlech TV had been to see her and when she said no they suggested that Robert Green had put her up to telling the story. Eighty-five years of age and in frail health, Constance became extremely distressed, finally signing a statement she still does not think properly covered what she had wanted to say.[7] At least she fared better than other friends of Hilda who offered help and information and were never seen at all. One close friend will play a crucial role later in this story.

Early in the summer it was being openly suggested among those who had known Hilda that her death had been in some way connected with the paper which was to have been delivered at Sizewell.

There was still no sign of such a theory surfacing in the official investigation, however. By the middle of May, the police had checked out 'thousands' of red Escorts and it was noted that a witness had come forward to say that one had been seen in the Haughmond Hill area on the day of the murder. Detective Superintendent Barry Mayne told reporters, 'There is no light at the end of the tunnel at this stage. We are still working through all the information we gained from the publicity in the early days of the inquiry. This will take us many months . . .' The confident predictions of catching the killer and nets closing in had ceased.

On 5 July the BBC's *Crimewatch* programme featured the Murrell murder, a subject to which they would return again the following spring. This was in the early days of the programme and the national media paid more attention to whether or not the idea of encouraging the public to 'solve' crimes was a good thing, than to its actual content. Outside the Shrewsbury area the story of the murder made little impact. To go with the programme, West Mercia Police produced a second 'artist's impression of the killer'. The first had been that of a square-jawed, fair-haired man, the second showed a thin-faced fellow with a shock of black hair and 'distinctive, deep-set eyes'. Neither fitted the police's initial verbal description.

Crimewatch did not provoke a flood of new information, but a lorry-driver from South Wales came forward to say he had picked up a male hitch-hiker at about the time witnesses had seen the running man. Nothing ever seems to have come of this.

There were still ninety-one regular police officers working on the case in July, but it was to transpire that from quite early on in the investigation not all the policemen who knocked on doors or took statements were ordinary members of the West Mercia police force. Some of them were from Special Branch.

Hilda's friend Joan Tate told me that summer, 'The Special Branch are definitely involved somewhere, but no one has been told in what way and why and whether they told the local police they were around.' Such Special Branch involvement is unusual, particularly as in this instance the police continued to reiterate that the murderer was an opportunist thief. The suggestion that Special Branch officers had joined the investigation and were posing as ordinary members of the CID was briskly discounted when it first surfaced and it was not until the December of that year that their involvement was officially confirmed when in the House of Commons Giles Shaw, Minister of State at the Home Office, told Tam Dalyell, 'It should be understood that specialist officers are often called upon to perform non-specialist roles when the manpower demands are great. This has been the situation in this case. Special Branch officers have been used in routine inquiry work.'

This was then confirmed by the Chief Constable of West Mercia, Robert Cozens. The appearance of Special Branch on the scene had been 'a routine measure since, generally speaking, local officers support local forces as part of operational procedures.' This prompted a letter to the *Guardian* from a Mrs Janet Evans of Woburn, Bucks:

'Obviously I'm glad to hear from Mr Cozens (who as Chief Constable of West Mercia should certainly know) that Special Branch officers were involved in the murder inquiry on a "routine" basis because of manpower demands; it is good to know that they sometimes spend their time on something more socially useful than bugging my phone.

'Now can somebody give me a list of the other "routine investigations" that Special Branch helped with during 1984 or was this the *only* case with no security implications that they chanced to be involved with?

'There is no reason for refusing to give me such a list because, if they were investigating ordinary murders, burglaries and suchlike, the information cannot be classified; and if they helped to solve any of these crimes, it is only right they should have the credit for it to improve their present – rather unfortunate – image.'

Surveillance expert Gary Murray states in his recent book *Enemies of the State* that it was not only middle- and lower-ranking officers that were involved, but that the Commanding Officer of Shrewsbury Special Branch also visited witnesses posing as a member of the CID.

Indeed, the police gave the impression there were no lengths to which they would not go to catch the killer. They even brought in the FBI.[8] Happily the FBI's 'profile' of the murderer agreed in almost every detail with that of West Mercia Police who were now confidently asserting that they were convinced – on information they could not release – that he was local, with intimate knowledge of the area, aged between thirty and thirty-five, of medium height, 'a loner who is probably being shielded by someone locally'.

The FBI's profile, on the basis of information from the West Mercia Police, was that he was in his thirties, a loner – again that magic word – and an 'unsocialised and withdrawn individual'. He was probably a habitué of licensed premises and was likely to be an unskilled worker. Chief Superintendent Cole, commenting on the FBI's report said, 'There is little doubt he made his way to Miss Murrell's house on foot and it is therefore likely he does not own a vehicle. It is also thought likely he may have some knowledge of the attacked premises where his motive was primarily burglary.'

Not all those involved in the investigation, however, felt themselves to be under such pressure that they needed extra help. In June 1984 three senior officers involved in the murder hunt were discovered to have been playing golf when they should have been pursuing their inquiries. As doubts about the progress of the investigation grew and questions began to arise as to whether or not there was another dimension to the murder, the suggestion was made that possibly the police had their own reasons for not wanting to pursue the killer with too much enthusiasm, as instanced by the golf-playing policemen.[9]

This provoked an angry reaction from the police. 'This is very far from true,' went the statment. 'Senior officers on the murder inquiry carrying out their supervisory duties became aware of discrepancies in these officers' duties and reported it to the Chief Constable, who implemented disciplinary measures and caused them to be suspended.'[10]

The inquest which had been set for 5 July was postponed until 24 October. Robert Green, meanwhile, had been trying to get hold of a copy of Acland's post mortem report on his aunt, but this had been refused. Indeed, it was refused for many months. He was informed, however, that while he could not be given any of the information in the report for operational reasons, he could ask questions about it and the police would try and answer them.

As Green said at the time, 'You can imagine our difficulties as, since we had no idea what was in it, we didn't know what to ask.' He did manage to discover, in a macabre version of Twenty Questions, that his aunt had had a broken collar-bone, small stab wounds in her stomach and had 'probably' died of hypothermia. When he asked about the disposal of the body, he was told there could be no question of it at that stage. It might have to be kept for months, years even, as it would be needed when the murderer was caught as it was expected he would be.

It therefore came as a shock when on 3 August Green was telephoned by Shrewsbury Police and told he must remove the body straight away as it was deteriorating rapidly. He was even more surprised when he was informed that a second autopsy had been carried out on 25 July by another pathologist. This was, said the police, necessary in case a second opinion was needed by a defence counsel when the murderer was brought to trial. Green was refused a copy of this report, too. It appears the coroner's refusal was wrong, as also was Giles Shaw when, in a House of Commons answer on 17 January 1985, he said, 'Turning to the availability to Miss Murrell's family of the post mortem report, the release of this on formal application is a matter entirely within the coroner's discretion and not one in which I would intervene.'

Inquest, the United Campaign for Justice, says, 'The supply of a post mortem report on formal application is covered by Rule 57 of the Coroners' Rules 1984 (S.I. No. 205). These Rules do not however apply to a post mortem conducted before July 1st 1984 and the relevant Rule is therefore Rule 39 of the Coroners' Rules 1953 (S.I. No. 205). Both these rules include the following words: "A coroner *shall* on application and on payment of the prescribed fee (if any) supply to any person who, in the opinion of the coroner, is a properly interested person, a copy of any report of a post mortem examination . . ."'

'The release of the post mortem is *not* "entirely within the Coroner's discretion" once he has decided that the applicant is a "properly interested person". The phrase "properly interested person" is also used to describe a person who is entitled to question witnesses at an inquest. It is very difficult to see how a coroner can acknowledge a person as "properly interested" in being represented at an inquest, but not in applying for a copy of the post mortem. We would argue that it is not within the coroner's lawful discretion to withhold the post mortem report from a person who is entitled to examine witnesses at the inquest, as defined by Rule 20 of the 1984 Rules. And so the family were entitled to receive a copy of the report, which might have gone some way to explaining the circumstances of Hilda Murrell's death. The disclosure of a report could not prejudice investigations – if these really were proceeding as police statements indicated.'

Green immediately contacted the hospital administrator who confirmed what the police had told him, adding that the hospital would like the body removed by 8 August as the space was needed. The 8th was a Sunday and Green asked the hospital to give him more time as it was such very short notice, he lived a considerable distance away and had to arrange matters with an undertaker.

There has never been an adequate explanation as to why the body had to be removed and cremated in such haste. Why had it deteriorated so badly in the controlled conditions of the mortuary that the police felt impelled to get rid of it? They admitted themselves they were no nearer catching the murderer.

The body in another notorious case, that of the British nurse Helen Smith, who was alleged to have died following a fall from a balcony during an illegal drinks party in Jeddah, survived the sweltering heat of Saudi Arabia before being flown home, where it was kept in a Leeds mortuary for years. Her body was subjected to no fewer than four autopsies and it was only the last of these that proved that she had been raped before death.

Hilda's family duly made arrangements for the funeral and the body was delivered in a zinc-lined coffin. They were advised not to look inside. On 25 August Hilda Murrell was cremated, any secrets her body might have held being consigned to the flames with her.

Chief Superintendent David Cole, who attended the service, told the *Shropshire Star* afterwards that he was still hopeful. Indeed, only in the last few days new information had come in as a result of extensive inquiries. Some 26,000 records were now in the computer system and were being analysed and checked. 'I am still confident,' he said, 'that the answer lies not far away or indeed in Shrewsbury itself.'

In spite of such reassurances there were those in Shrewsbury who had been convinced, almost from the outset, that the answer did not lie close to home but a good deal further away; that Hilda, either by accident or design, had been the victim of something a good deal more sinister than a simple burglary followed by assault.

The first theory to emerge and which was now gathering increasing strength was that somehow it might have something to do with her involvement as a protester at the Sizewell Inquiry. This can be described as 'the nuclear connection'.

The second, far more dramatic and remarkable, concerned the events surrounding the sinking of the Argentine battleship *General Belgrano* during the Falklands conflict and the subsequent high-level cover-up, 'the *Belgrano* connection'.

What makes the Murrell murder a unique case is that it is highly likely that these two apparently disparate strands, her history of anti-nuclear protest and a high level government cover-up in the aftermath of the Falklands War, became inextricably bound together by a fortuitous and bizarre set of circumstances brought about by the political climate of the time.

PART II

The Politics

Chapter 5

'One of us . . .'

'Where there is discord, may we bring harmony. . .' So went the first line of the cod 'prayer of St Francis' spoken by Margaret Thatcher on the steps of 10 Downing Street as she took office, a prayer which arguably ushered in the era of the most confrontational politician ever elected Prime Minister.

Acres of comment from political columnists and the memoirs of dozens of senior politicians, including her own, have chronicled the Thatcher years. The politicians, not surprisingly, differed widely according to their own points of view. Opinions remain deeply divided. On the one hand are those who believe monetarism was a tremendous success, that we really did have an economic miracle, that the destruction of the country's manufacturing base led to a leaner, fitter Britain, that rolling back the frontiers of the welfare state has led to the good life all round (give or take the odd hiccup), that we are better off with privatised utilities and a decayed transport infrastructure, and that there is no such thing as society. On the other hand there are those who profoundly disagree, who point to the balance of payments deficit caused, in no small part, by the loss of manufacturing capacity, to the underclass which has emerged in the wastelands of the inner cities, to a two-tier health service, to demoralised teachers, to poor, expensive public tranport and a rising crime rate, and ask was it worth it?

On one point both sides would agree: that Margaret Thatcher, who mercilessly criticised the Cabinet colleagues she herself chose and who berated them for lack of loyalty, saw almost every situation in simple terms of them and us. Whether she was taking on the 'wets' in her Cabinet, the National Union of Mineworkers, loyal trade unionists at GCHQ Cheltenham or the bishops, it was a fight to the death. As Hugo Young explains in his seminal work on the Thatcher years, *One of Us*[1], she had coined that phrase long before she became Prime Minister. To be admitted to the charmed circle of those so designated, it was necessary to offer unstinting loyalty to herself and her cause, whatever the cost.

Ex-diplomat Sir Anthony Parsons, interviewed on 20 October 1993 in a BBC television programme made, along with many others, to mark the publication of the Thatcher memoirs, recalled how early in her 'reign' she confided to him that 'there are people in our own party who actually believe in consensus'. 'I said to her,' Sir Anthony told viewers, 'I am a consensus man myself. I've believed in it ever since I can remember.' She gave him a frosty look. '*I* call them quislings and traitors!'

'In her mind, of course,' writes Sir Ian Gilmour in his recent book *Dancing with Dogma*[2], '"conviction" was diametrically opposed to "consensus".' To those of us outside senior Conservative circles, Gilmour's description of the early Thatcher years is of a loyalty test of belief in monetarism being demanded of Cabinet members much in the way Henry VIII decreed that all the members of his Privy Council should swear an oath recognising his marriage to Anne Boleyn and himself as Head of the Church. 'Following Mrs Thatcher's election to the party leadership in 1975,' continues Gilmour, 'many other Conservative politicians were also born again, some of them overnight. Those who resisted conversion and clung instead to traditional Tory principles were soon regarded as, at best, suspect infidels or, at worst, the enemy within.'

Certainly the term 'enemy within', adopted by Mrs Thatcher, came to mean anyone with whom Thatcher disagreed – the unions, 'do-gooders', anyone who stood in the way of the new radical politics. It was an era when legitimate opposition was considered at best subversive and at worst, as she told Parsons, treasonable.

It is not surprising, therefore, given such a climate, that the security services which in this country have never been properly accountable, had a field day. MI5, as we know from ex-members who decided to blow the whistle, were set on not just to monitor those suspected of espionage or terrorism but so-called 'soft' targets, members of CND, the National Council for Civil Liberties (as it then was), trade unions and ecological pressure groups. Thatcher's love affair with the nuclear deterrent and the arrival of Cruise missiles from America put anyone who was against either nuclear weapons, nuclear power or both at the forefront of those considered the enemy within.

With such an attitude goes a love of secrecy, which meant that, far from answering the calls for a proper re-think of the Official Secrets Act, as had been called for by the Franks Committee set up to look into its workings, and for a complementary Freedom of Information Act, we ended up with the worst of all worlds: another badly drafted Official Secrets Act with no compensatory Freedom of Information legislation and a morass of 'charters' instead of access to basic, ordinary information. We stand almost alone in the developed world in not having a Freedom of Information Act – what is a natural right for Americans, Australians, the Dutch, French, Germans, Belgians, Scandinavians and others is too dangerous for the Brits. On the coat tails of the official security services hang the rag-tag of private investigation agencies from those at the upmarket end owned by members of the establishment, ex-MI5 and-MI6 staff, the old boy network and suchlike, and at the bottom end by very doubtful operators, some with criminal records.

Should we worry that we may be the object of either official or unofficial surveillance? Well, according to a report in the *Guardian* on 18 April 1984 – a month after Hilda's death – some 500,000 of us at that time had our names stored on file in the old MI5 building in London. By 1991, according to intelligence expert Richard Norton-Taylor in *In Defence of the Realm*, published by the then National Council for Civil Liberties, the number had grown to 700,000. Have these folders containing documents, photographs and typed records of our beliefs, activities, friends, families, jobs and homes, and allegations of suspicions about us been moved to the new MI5 building on Millbank? Or is all the information now stored in the new MI5 computer, capacity 20 million files? According to Norton-Taylor 'actual files on individuals number about one million'. Either we have the most subversive population in the world which, on present showing, is extremely doubtful, or something is badly wrong with the system.

A whole section of MI5, known as F Branch, is devoted solely to 'domestic subversion'. Among 'targets' known to have been monitored in the past by F Division and, indeed, by Special Branch, are the Woodcraft Folk – the children's section of the Co-operative movement – hunt saboteurs, the organisers of a ball at Keele University and an entire class studying Marxism and Literature at Gwent College of Further Education.

Those who attempt to blow the whistle on MI5 activities do not fare well as is instanced by the case of Cathy Massiter, the former MI5 agent who resigned from its F Branch after she felt she could no longer continue in an organisation which was targeting legitimate opposition. Because of the furore over the arrival of the American Cruise Missiles at Greenham Common in Berkshire, there had been an enormous upsurge of anti-nuclear protest, particularly among women. Both Margaret Thatcher and Michael Heseltine, then Minister of Defence, were loud in their condemnation of such opposition and MI5 was set on to carry out surveillance of protesters. The row over Massiter's resignation revelations and appearance in Channel 4's

Twenty-Twenty Vision programme in mid–March 1985 made it apparent that by the mid 1980s the term 'subversive' could literally mean just about anyone who held legitimate opposing views to government policy. Targets for surveillance ranged from individuals to whole organisations, however respectable and official, and it is worth noting here that the number of phone taps officially recorded as having been granted by a Home Secretary gives no idea of the true scale, as one warrant can be given to cover an entire organisation such as a trade union, e.g. the miners during the Miners' Strike, or members of CND.

Regional Officers of MI5 provide a direct link between the organisation and each local Special Branch. In the August following Hilda's death, Duncan Campbell, writing in the *New Statesman*, discussed the purpose and activities of MI5's A (Operations) Branch.[3] Until then this information had been so secret it was not even revealed to the Cabinet and Home Office officials supposed to supervise the internal activities of MI5. 'The purpose of this secrecy,' wrote Campbell, 'is to enable ministers and orthodox civil servants to continue to deny any knowledge that MI5 breaks the law as it applies to others, with impunity.' According to Campbell, under this control comes the AIA branch which is responsible for illicitly gathering information, transcribing both legal and illegal phone taps and organising illegal break-ins. MPs have complained, without success, about the apparent *carte blanche* this group has to break the law in any way that suits it, which, wrote Campbell, 'has frequently been demonstrated by break-ins against political groups'. He continues, somewhat prophetically since the story of the events surrounding Hilda's murder had not yet broken, 'Although members . . . have so far escaped public prosecution on the occasions the police have caught them at their work, it can only be a matter of time before an MI5 burglary goes wrong.' In the event, it was not an AIA break-in in Hilda's case although the theory behind it was similar.

MI5 has, of course, had something of an image problem since the publication of *Spycatcher* by ex–MI5 officer Peter Wright.[4] In it he explained how freewheeling souls within the organisation had tried their best to bring down the democratically elected Labour government of Harold Wilson. Wright became the focus for one of Margaret Thatcher's personal vendettas. Her efforts to prevent the publication of the memoirs first in Australia then, when that failed, in Britain, cost the taxpayer tens of thousands of pounds and led to her Cabinet Secretary, Sir Robert Armstrong, reinventing the phrase which reverberated around the world, 'being economical with the truth'. (The original coining of the phrase is variously ascribed to St Thomas Aquinas or Edmund Burke.) Whatever one feels about Wright, and the answer might well be 'not a lot', one has at least to recognise that he took Thatcher on and won.

But most often the work of monitoring 'soft targets' goes to the Special Branch. Officially the Special Branch is not a national body but is made up of individual officers from the different police forces under the control of the chief constables of each area. Shrewsbury had its own Special Branch office. Special Branch lards its activities with exotic names. 'Still Life' is the name given to the collection of membership lists of organisations considered worthy of surveillance, 'Azure Blue' to personal surveillance.

During hearings before the Commons' Home Affairs Committee in January 1985, the head of Scotland Yard's Special Branch told the committee that its job was to 'help the security forces defend the realm'. Deputy Assistant Commissioner Colin Hewitt said that one aspect of the work carried out by the 400 members of his Special Branch was assessing the strengths of demonstrations. Records of possible 'subversives' were kept on computer, not on file – at that time. He denied that all anti-nuclear supporters were automatically logged, although he refused to say just how many were on file as 'this would be against the public interest'.

The Chief Constable of Northamptonshire, Mr Maurice Buck, told the committee that his force only employed seven Special Branch men out of a thousand officers, but that they held between 400 and 500 files. Mr Kenneth Oxford, then Chief Constable of Merseyside, said his branch was made up of 178 officers out of 4,700 policemen and that they kept 'several hundreds, possibly thousands of records'. He also admitted that Special Branch information had sometimes leaked out to unauthorised people but that these rare occurrences were regretted. His computer, however, had fewer names on it than it had had two years previously.

So could Hilda have been of interest to the various branches of the security services on the basis of her anti-nuclear activity alone? Indeed she could. MI5 had blanket permission to carry out surveillance on anti-nuclear protesters and Hilda was either a member of, or was sympathetic to, a raft of organisations which would have come within their remit, from the Nuclear Freeze Advertising Campaign to the Shropshire Peace Alliance and Shrewsbury Peace Group. She took part in the 1983 anti-Cruise demonstration and she wrote letters on nuclear policy, military and civil, to national newspapers.

If anyone thinks that is insufficient to attract the attention of, at the very least, Special Branch, then one can only point to the experience of a Mrs Madeleine Haigh who in 1981 wrote a letter to a local weekly paper, the *Solihull News*, in which she expressed herself as being against the siting of Cruise missiles in Britain whilst also condemning violent demonstrations. During the next little while she was visited on no fewer than three occasions by policemen posing as members of the local CID, wishing to question her about a mail-order fraud perpetrated not only in her name but from her address. Inexplicably, the telephone would ring in the small hours of the morning but when she went to answer it the line went dead. She began to notice men parked in cars outside her house which was in an isolated position and where she spent much time alone. Telephone conversations with friends were often interrupted also by the line going dead.

Thoroughly alarmed and unable to get any sense out of anyone as to why this was happening, she sought legal advice and announced she would be taking a complaint to the European Commission on Human Rights against the UK government for breaching her right to hold opinions and to receive and impart information and ideas without interference by public authorities. She did not, however, expect to get very far.

Suddenly, after eight months of effort, she wrenched from the then Chief Constable of the West Midlands Police, Sir Philip Knight, the admission that she had been under investigation by Special Branch as a direct result of writing her letter to the *Solihull News*. Commenting on the matter at the same Commons' Home Affairs Committee hearings already mentioned, Kenneth Oxford said that such surveillance had possibly been 'over zealous, but there are a lot of zealous police officers'. In a statement made four years later, Mrs Haigh said, 'My request to each anti-nuclear campaigner reading this is, please don't let them get away with anything in your life. If we try to protect freedom in the little space we occupy individually, maybe we can collectively keep a big space free enough for better days to come. The alternative is too terrible to contemplate.'[5] A sentiment with which Hilda Murrell would have heartily concurred. I will deal later with my own experiences of being under surveillance.

To return to the practicalities of surveillance: when, for whatever reason, clandestine entry is required – the most frequent reason is a search for documents – it is usual for MI5's AIA unit and Special Branch to combine on the operation. It would seem that the concern over such a burglary going wrong has not been confined to those who dislike the whole idea of such activity; it also extends to those who carry the operations out. They are told to proceed with great caution and are instructed not to steal anything, even if this draws attention to the fact that while a house has been broken into and searched, nothing of real value has been taken. Presumably this advice is also given to freelance teams operating either directly for MI5 or Special Branch or via a 'respectable' private investigatory intermediary.

If, however, something material has to be stolen, then Special

Branch is used, as well as a policeman who takes the item away and can then claim he had a warrant (issued retrospectively) to search the house, thus informing the local police force what is going on before the owner of the property contacts them.

The last organisation which keeps an eye on anti-nuclear protest, civil as well as military, is the United Kingdom Atomic Energy Special Constabulary, known colloquially as 'the nuclear police'. The nuclear police are so secret that MI5, MI6 and Special Branch are open books by comparison. They are so secret that we do not know how many of them there are. In 1985 the number was estimated vaguely at somewhere between 500 and a thousand. They have their own Chief Constable, whose annual report is a classified document, and everyone who joins has to go through a rigorous security vetting by our old MI5 and Special Branch.

It is one of life's ironies that this super-secret police force should have been given their wide-ranging and almost unlimited extra powers by that champion of accountability and democracy, Tony Benn. He also gave us the THORP reprocessing plant, now the cause of so much controversy. When he became Energy Minister in 1976, he gave the nuclear police power to carry a wide assortment of weapons, travel well outside the areas immediately surrounding nuclear installations, doing both by having a special clause inserted into the 1976 Special Constables Act, adding that a member could exercise his powers 'in any place where it appears to him expedient to go'. Their prime function, however, is to guard nuclear installations and nuclear waste on its way from the power stations to Sellafield, but what else might come within their remit we do not know nor is it possible to find out.

However, there is no good reason why the UKAEA police should have had anything whatsoever to do with Hilda Murrell. Nor is there one for saying that she was personally targeted for murder because she had acquired sensational material on nuclear power or nuclear weapons which has never come to light. It is obvious from her proposed Sizewell paper, well reasoned and carefully researched as it is, that all the information contained in it could have been assembled equally well by any other assiduous researcher. She had contacts with knowledge of the civil or military use of nuclear power, to whom she might have applied for assistance, but none of them had worked professionally in the field for years. It is, therefore, even less likely that she had somehow happened on information unknown to specialists investigating the subject. Yet for all that, it is possible that her journey towards disaster began because of her sympathy for anti-nuclear causes, even though that was not the reason for its tragic end.

Chapter 6

The Nuclear Connection

At 10 a.m. on Tuesday 23 October 1979 a meeting of the Cabinet Committee on Economic Strategy was called at 10 Downing Street. It was presided over by the Prime Minister and the Cabinet members chosen to attend were Lord Carrington (Foreign Secretary), Geoffrey Howe (Chancellor of the Exchequer), Sir Keith Joseph (Industry), James Prior (Employment), Michael Heseltine (Environment), David Howell (Energy), Lord Soames (Lord President of the Council), Peter Walker (Agriculture, Fisheries and Food), John Nott (Department of Trade) and John Biffen (Chief Secretary to the Treasury). Also present were George Younger (Scottish Secretary), Attorney General Sir Michael Havers QC, and the Cabinet Secretary, Sir Robert Armstrong.

Margaret Thatcher was to bring the use of Cabinet Committees to a fine art, often using them to by-pass discussion in full Cabinet. To quote Sir Ian Gilmour again: 'Instead of trying to achieve a consensus in Cabinet, thus bringing harmony where there had been discord as she had recently promised, the Prime Minister governed by clique and committee, where "conviction" could have its head.' Mrs Thatcher, he continues, 'in the words of one commentator was uniquely unsuited to

61

Cabinet government and, therefore, removed the most vital aspects of policy-making from Cabinet discussion'.

The subject of this particular meeting was nuclear power and its place in general economic strategy. Within a relatively short time the minutes of its deliberations were widely leaked. These *were* early days.

The Prime Minister had already made her enthusiasm for nuclear power clear – she wanted to embark on a massive new programme, no less than ten nuclear power stations coming on stream in ten years, the first as early as 1983. It might be thought that someone would immediately have pointed out that such a notion was ludicrous and totally impractical. Nobody did.

Some of the Ministers present must have had knowledge of the past history of Britain's nuclear power programme and the massive problems that had beset it, from getting the nuclear reactors up and running to bringing the power stations finally on stream. If they did not know themselves then they had plenty of civil servants in the relevant departments who could have briefed them, not only on the apparently endless delays on each and every station but also as to the routine massive over-run with regard to costs. To prove the point, it is possible to pick almost any site at random, and Dungeness B is a good example. There was already an ageing Magnox nuclear power station, Dungeness A, on the site when in 1965 the decision was taken to build a second nuclear station next to it, but this time to go for a new type of nuclear reactor, the advanced gas-cooled reactor (AGR). A number of consortia tendered and surprise was expressed when the Central Electricity Generating Board (CEGB) chose Atomic Power Constructions, as it had been far from satisfied with the work the company had carried out at another nuclear power station, Trawsfynydd in North Wales.

The CEGB estimated the cost would be £87.5 million. From the start the building of Dungeness B was dogged by design problems and the discovery of construction faults. Meanwhile Dungeness A plodded on, beset by troubles. In March 1979 it was found necessary to repair cracks up to one metre long in the welding of a gas bellows for the primary cooling circuit close to the very core of the reactor. During a routine biennial inspection, the CEGB had cleared the reactor as safe and it was only because the Nuclear Inspectorate disagreed that a more thorough examination was carried out and more cracks were discovered. The reactor had to be shut down for four days at an estimated cost of £4 million. By January 1980, nuclear engineers were telling *Nature* magazine that they despaired of Dungeness A ever working properly. Finally, towards the end of 1982 Dungeness B limped on stream well below capacity – it had taken nearly eighteen years and its cost had escalated to £587 million. The *Daily Telegraph*, announcing the news, called Dungeness B 'the worst ever advert for the nuclear and construction industries'.[1]

It was a story familiar to critics of nuclear power. The new power station at Hartlepool had come on stream nine years late and at a cost of £520 million, five times its original estimate.[2]

Such hiccups were not, however, allowed to dent the optimism of the Cabinet Committee discussion that October morning. First David Howell outlined the position. A substantial nuclear programme was essential to the nation's long-term energy needs. To that end he had provided each member with a paper proving that the cost of nuclear power was likely to be significantly below that of alternative fuels 'with the calculations robust against significant adverse movements in the assumptions'. If progress were to be made it was vital to have a vigorous nuclear construction industry and for this it was important that the industry had faith in the government's commitment to nuclear power. It was therefore proposed that the government should embark on an ambitious programme using a different type of reactor from that used hitherto – the pressurised water reactor (PWR). A licensing agreement already drawn up with the American company Westinghouse would be activated and detailed designs prepared for a British PWR.

There was, say the minutes, 'general support for the concept of a substantial nuclear programme and for the inclusion in that programme of PWRs'. Interestingly enough, in view of what has happened recently, they go on to note that 'such a programme would not reduce the long-term requirement for coal, because of the likely decline in world oil supplies towards the end of the century. But a nuclear programme would have the advantage of removing a substantial portion of electricity production from the dangers of disruption by coal miners or transport workers.'

At this point one of the participants, it is not clear who, ventured the remark that there were 'substantial problems in achieving a nuclear power programme, not the least of which was opposition which might provide a focus for protest groups over the next decade'. The government might, therefore, make more rapid progress towards its objective by ensuring a low-profile approach to the new nuclear programme. Howell's response was that the existing stations had a long record of safe operation and 'lots of people near the various nuclear sites were very content with them'.

It was then that the dreaded words 'Three Mile Island' were uttered. On 16 March 1979 a Hollywood thriller had opened in the main New York Cinemas. It was called *The China Syndrome* and it starred Jack Lemmon as the manager of a power station with a PWR. The plot hinged on a disastrous accident, followed by a cover-up. Within hours of the film's first showings, the American nuclear industry rushed out press releases to the effect that such an accident was impossible, it simply couldn't happen. On 28 March, just twelve days later, it did. The story of Three Mile Island has been thoroughly documented, thanks to the US Freedom of Information Act, but suffice it to say that what became known as 'the night we nearly lost Pennsylvania' was still fresh in people's minds at the time the Cabinet Committee were discussing a massive nuclear expansion programme in Britain using American Westinghouse PWRs. The emergence of Three Mile Island as a topic caused some concern and it was agreed that there might well be a problem in maintaining the desired low profile once a decision was made to proceed with a PWR, even though it had a different design to that which had run amok in Pennsylvania earlier in the year.

Howell did point out that the new programme could not be implemented as quickly as might be wished because of the statutory duty to hold public inquiries. Such inquiries took time to set up, due to the procedural problems involved, and he did not think the first could even begin its hearings until 1981. He also thought it arguable that the first inquiry, at least, should be wide-ranging, in order to establish the broad facts of the system, although he hoped its findings would save time when it came to subsequent inquiries. It was however pointed out that there was always a danger that a truly broad-ranging inquiry 'would arouse prolonged technical debate between representatives of different facets of scientific opinion'. This, and the fact that the development of the new programme would have to include identifying new sites for the disposal of nuclear waste, also requiring Public Inquiries might well 'provide a focus for protest groups'.

The meeting concluded with the Prime Minister's brisk summing up. It was agreed, therefore, she said, that the government should aim to achieve a sizeable nuclear programme which included PWRs. A balance between PWRs and other types of reactor would be the subject of later discussions. The committee also agreed proposals for restructuring the nuclear industry and enhancing the role of the National Nuclear Corporation as set out in Howell's paper. The importance of appropriate 'presentation' for achieving the government's objective was agreed and the 'low-profile approach' favoured. David Howell would consult Michael Heseltine when preparing his proposals for handling the presentation of the massive new programme.

'The Committee took note, with approval, of the summing up of their discussion by the Prime Minister and invited the Secretary of State for Energy, the Secretary of State for the Environment and the Secretary of State for Trade to be guided [by her] accordingly.'

* * *

So far from a new nuclear power station being built and on stream by 1983, it had taken that long just to set up the first public inquiry, that to be held at Sizewell in Suffolk into the building of Sizewell B, which David Howell had confidently assumed would be under-way by 1981 at the latest.

Throughout 1982 opponents of the scheme marshalled their forces and in the winter of 1982/83 someone somewhere decided to set up a large and complex intelligence operation to undertake the surveillance of all individuals and groups concerning themselves with the proposed building of Sizewell B. It has always been denied that it was authorised by any government department. We do know from Cathy Massiter among others that in the early 1980s various departments, especially Defence and the Home Office, were actively monitoring anti-nuclear war protesters via MI5 and, according to a report in the *Guardian* in October 1993,[3] Mrs Thatcher herself took a personal interest in the covert investigation of the Peace Studies Department of Bradford University during the same period.

Professor James O'Connell, head of the department from 1979 to September 1993, said in a lecture on his retirement that 'Pressure mounted and it was eventually intimated that the government wanted us investigated. Although staff members in Peace Studies considered that government intervention of this kind broke accepted conventions and violated academic freedom, we were sure that we had nothing to hide and were prepared to be investigated.' So we know that the government was directly involved in these two areas at least.

It is difficult to imagine who else would have had the authority to mount such an operation. One suggestion made at the time was that it was the CEGB, but there are no grounds, on available evidence, for supposing this was the case, though they might well have been happy to use any information passed on to them. No one has ever admitted to ordering the surveillance, although some months after Hilda's death information from an 'informed source' was circulated to a number of reporters, including Gareth Parry of the *Guardian*[4], that 'a foreign company which builds nuclear reactors was yesterday believed likely to be the client of a consultancy firm which used a private detective agency to discover information about objectors appearing at the Sizewell power station inquiry'. No trace of this shadowy foreign outfit has ever been discovered and it is unlikely to be a coincidence that the information appeared within hours of reports published in the media as to the identity of the security firms involved.

Whoever authorised the operation, late in 1982 the private security firm Zeus Securities was chosen to organise the surveillance. Zeus, which had excellent establishment connections and a track record for assisting the government, was owned by Peter Hamilton, a former director of Chubb Security Services with a background in intelligence. His work has taken him to China (in 1943) and Malaya and in a private capacity as Security Officer to the Cyprus government, followed by a period as Security Adviser to the old white Rhodesian government. In 1979 he became Chairman of the European Chapter of the American Society for Industrial Security.[5] He also admits to have undertaken work for the Economic League, an outfit which became notorious for the inaccurate information on innocent individuals it purveyed to private and government organisations, information which all too often led to the blacklisting of workers.

The world of security is confusing, for some people own more than one investigation agency while directly employing within these concerns investigators with small companies of their own. During this time the day-to-day running of Zeus was in the hands of one Jeremy Wetherall, who also had a share in another security firm, Lynx. Wetherall took an honours degree in law, followed by service in the Metropolitan Police and British Intelligence. His c.v. states that he was a senior kidnap negotiations adviser, operating in both political and criminal cases.

Hamilton, who also owned Peter Hamilton (Security Consultants) Ltd, had some prestigious colleagues. One was

Lord Chalfont. According to Liberal Democrat leader Paddy Ashdown MP in a question to Mrs Thatcher in 1989, 'at the time of the instigation of the Sizewell operation, Lord Chalfont was Chairman of Zeus Security Consultants Ltd. As at April 1988 he is named as Consultant on the headed note-paper of Peter Hamilton (Security Consultants) Ltd.' Mr Ashdown was querying the suitability of Lord Chalfont to be Deputy Chairman of the Independent Broadcasting Authority.[6]

Both Zeus and Lord Chalfont have made it clear that they had nothing whatever to do with the Hilda Murrell affair and the latter sued the *Observer* for suggesting that this might possibly be so even at a remove. Most references are, therefore, taken from statements made in Parliament.

Other consultants included Major General Sir Philip Ward KCVO CBE, a former army officer, and the leading City banker, Sir Dallas Bernard. Sir Dallas had contacts at a very high level, being on friendly terms with the Cabinet Secretary, Sir Robert Armstrong; indeed Armstrong stood godfather to his daughter at her christening at the Royal Chapel, Windsor, on 11 July 1981.

Quoting Paddy Ashdown again, the Articles of Association of Zeus include, 'To carry on business as security experts and agents of all kinds and to provide advisory and consultancy services to Government and other Authorities and to encourage the adoption of security and precautionary measures and devices against industrial and other espionage'.[7]

From 1984 onwards questions were regularly asked in Parliament as to just what the relationship was between Zeus and government departments. The result is a plethora of answers, nearly all of which fall into two unhelpful categories – 'information on this subject is not readily available and could be provided only at disproportionate cost', and 'I am not aware the MoD has had any dealings with either of the companies quoted', etc. However on 23 May 1988 David Mellor had said, in a reply to Labour MP Ken Livingstone and after giving the ritual response as to the disproportionate cost involved in providing information, that Zeus had been employed 'six years ago and on two further occasions in 1983'. He did not proffer any information as to the nature of the work undertaken in 1983.[8]

However, Zeus did not undertake the Sizewell surveillance itself. It put the work out to another security company, the Sapphire Investigation Bureau Ltd, run by a man called Barry Peachman from his base at Acle, near Norwich. Hamilton himself rang Peachman at 7.13 p.m. on 21 January 1983 and gave him the job. Peachman was asked to find out the names and backgrounds of the principal objectors, their connections and their political colour. Investigations should be wide-ranging, taking in both outside objectors and local people who might well be acting as frontmen for other organisations. Hamilton and Peachman were to contact each other mainly by telephone and Peachman duly kept a note of subsequent conversations.[9]

Unlike Hamilton, Peachman had no background in intelligence or security work before forming his own company. Surprisingly, in view of the size of Zeus's proposed operation, Sapphire was an extremely small firm, staffed by Peachman's wife, Jean, and utilising his two grown-up sons, while his co-director was Shirley Smith, his long-term mistress and mother of his nine-year-old son. It might also have been assumed that such a set-up was bound, of its very nature, to cause strain, as Peachman divided his time between wife and mistress.

It is obvious that Peachman would need help and on 26 January he duly rang Hamilton, first leaving a message on his Ansaphone, then speaking to him in person when he explained 'we were using an investigator outside of our regular staff, etc. Agrees we should get company searches. Told inquiries continuing and would be in touch. Only question he [Hamilton] raised was if I knew what paper Jennifer Armitage was with?'

The following day he rang Hamilton again, after initiating some company searches, and noted that although 'the client is Zeus, we send reports just addressed to P.R. Hamilton, Driftway, Badwell Ash, Bury St Edmunds, Suffolk'.

On 31 January the identity of the outside investigator became apparent. 'Vic Norris phoned, claims he can put a stopper on CND if required, will send further report.'[10]

This is where the sleaze really starts. Vic Norris or Adrian Hampson or Adrian Page, whichever name he chose to use, also ran a private investigation agency, Contingency Services, based in Colchester. He had, to put it mildly, a remarkable background, for this agency was only one of his many interests. He also ran AH Services, a mail-order Nazi memorabilia service (the initials are those of Adolf Hitler), had organised two extreme right-wing groups, the 5000 Group and the Salvo Society, and, some years previously, had founded the Anglian Satanic Church. As if that was not enough, in 1969 he was convicted of a string of child sex offences, one of which involved his own daughters and another procuring under-age young girls for his friends. For that he served four years of a six-year term.[11] Norris/Hampson openly bragged about how useful he was to more august bodies who used him for the kind of work with which they did not wish to sully themselves.

On 31 January he wrote to Peachman discussing a recent telephone conversation and enclosing a note of names and addresses of Sizewell objectors. He also informed him that under the name of A. Page he had asked for an official list of Sizewell objectors and that it was on its way subject only to bureaucratic delays. This is where his activities become almost farcical, since *anyone* can find out such official information. Any half-intelligent fifth-former could have done so, let alone a private investigation agency. When Norris did receive the list from the inquiry bureau, he blundered around like Inspector Clouseau, seeking information on organisations which was readily obtainable from their press officers and listing subversive objectors, at least two of whom were almost certainly working on the same side as himself.[12]

There are, however, more unpleasant undertones. In the

January letter to Peachman he says, 'With regard to the rather spectacular news I mentioned briefly on the telephone, this could be really big money, so it will be interesting to see how your principals react. I think you will agree that it would be best now if, until you hear from your principals on what further action to take, I hold off from further investigation other than any information which is due to come to me by post, which I will immediately forward to you.'

Two weeks later he wrote thanking Peachman for a cheque for £67.30. 'You ask if this is satisfactory and I can assure you it is, and I had every confidence that it would be.'

He then goes on to enlarge on what he 'mentioned to Shirley when she telephoned'. That is that he had felt it useful to set up three dummy organisations apparently sympathetic to CND, 'all three run by trusted friends of mine'. One is in Lancashire, one in Kirkcaldy and the third in Ipswich. He did not know how useful this would be but his instinct had prompted him to go ahead, particularly in Ipswich where the bogus group had made contact with anti-nuclear protesters. He continues, 'The main point being that, if the principals for whom you are acting lose interest, we must consider that there are other [wealthy] sources who have a vested interest in seeing CND discredited and perhaps we could look elsewhere for potential clients?'

Outside he was more expansive, telling a supposed potential client that he specialised in 'delicate work', continuing, 'We have a couple of very good imitation lefties. They know the score. They know the patois these people use. They can drop names. They have connections. We can infiltrate all right. We do the work the Home Office don't want their own people to do.'

Meanwhile Peachman was assiduously passing on information to Zeus, including that so easily obtained by Norris, listing organisations from the National Union of Mineworkers to Friends of the Earth. Some of these, reported Peachman, were objecting 'on economic grounds. Others for genuine environmental or conservation reasons.' Particular note was being taken of a number of anti-nuclear groups. 'There are scores of anti-nuclear alliance groups preceded by the name of their town and district.' The examples he gives are those of Cornwall and Welsh Anti-Nuclear Alliances.

A second letter follows up the query regarding 'Jennifer Armitage', who turns out to be Jennifer Armstrong, secretary of the East Anglian Alliance Against Nuclear Power, 'who is covering the Sizewell B inquiry as a journalist'. In fact she was an employee of the Town and Country Planning Association. Peachman has verbal confirmation that there is 'close co-operation and concerted action between a number of these political groups'. Among the organisations Norris targeted was Friends of the Earth, whose sinister 'landlord is the Joseph Rowntree Social Services Trust, notorious for its financial help to dubious organisations . . .'

Over the years a number of worthy organisations have been given a start in life in low-rental office accommodation at 9 Poland Street, London, premises owned by the Rowntree Trust. Among these was indeed Friends of the Earth in its earliest days and also such subversive bodies as Gingerbread, the pressure group for one-parent families, Child Poverty Action and the Low Pay Unit. As an example of Norris's investigative abilities it is worth noting that the Rowntree Trust had long since ceased to be the landlord of Friends of the Earth which had moved on to larger premises three years earlier.

'We can provide numerous examples of the interlinking and overlapping of these various organisations,' he wrote. 'We can, if necessary, give examples of "paper organisations" with, perhaps, only one or two members, which are controlled by the primary organisations, and can give many other instances where individuals connected with one of the organisations are also closely connected with others.'[13]

However fatuous this might sound, it is important, for during the intense speculation in the aftermath of Hilda's death and when the role of the private investigative agencies was finally uncovered, much was made of the fact that her name had never appeared specifically on any of their lists. But this need not have been necessary for she was, as we know, a member of the Shropshire Anti-Nuclear Alliance and all such organisations were now under surveillance. She also had 'interlinking and overlapping' connections with others similarly in the firing line.

So, during 1983, while Hilda was busy on her Sizewell paper, a substantial number of objectors and protesters were under surveillance. That is a fact. It is also a fact that it is not possible to prove that she was specifically targeted. Questioned in 1985 about the Sizewell surveillance, Peter Hamilton confirmed that he had organised the operation (he could hardly do otherwise since there was now documentary evidence), suggesting first that it had been mounted to find 'subversives who were agitating'. Later he said he had been working for a private client. 'I can assure you this had nothing to do with Whitehall.'[14]

Vic Norris, who had had so much to say about his dummy peace groups and unspecified work for the Home Office, pedalled briskly backwards when questioned later, informing a reporter from the *Star* that he had only worked on Sizewell surveillance for one morning, 'an hour and a half of actual work'[15]. That this is manifestly untrue can be seen from the reports he was sending in to Sapphire Investigations.

Barry Peachman of Sapphire Investigations was unavailable for comment. On Tuesday 17 April, three weeks after Hilda's murder, he was found sitting in his car. A .410 shotgun was in his mouth and he had blown half his head off. The subsequent inquest was told that he had been under intense emotional strain owing to an extra-marital relationship with another woman. The impression given was that of a recent involvement.

But, as we know, it was not quite like that. Shirley Smith, as well as being Peachman's mistress and a co-director of Sapphire Investigations, virtually ran his office; not only had his relationship with her lasted some eleven years, but both it and the paternity of Shirley's son were an open secret, known not only to his family but to most people living nearby as well. The only possible clue is that on 2 April Shirley Smith had suddenly resigned from Sapphire for personal reasons.

According to Gary Murray, Peachman had been suffering from severe strain in the early part of April 1984 and had contacted him several times by telephone complaining that he seemed to be under surveillance and that the cars belonging to both Shirley Smith and himself appeared to have been tampered with. Apparently Vic Norris had also received such calls, telling Murray at the time that on one occasion Peachman had been 'virtually incoherent' but had not mentioned Shirley Smith's name once. Peachman had, however, told Murray that there were problems over his relationship with his mistress, and that this and other matters made him feel that he had his 'back against the wall'.

On the morning of his death Peachman had gone to London to meet Murray to discuss his problems but the meeting never took place. Murray says he found he could not make it as something else had cropped up.[16] Peachman returned to Norwich at 6.30 p.m. and made a number of telephone calls, one to Shirley Smith, after which he got in his car, drove it to her bungalow and went in to see her. He then returned to his car and shot himself.

Chapter 7

The Belgrano Connection

'This afternoon I knew what fear was. At 1400 (1800 London time), we received a signal authorising us to sink the cruiser *Belgrano*, even though it was outside our Exclusion Zone. We had been trailing her for more than twenty-five hours and held her visually at PO [periscope observation].

'After tracking her a while, we went into action stations around 1500 (1900 London time) and shut off for attack. The tension in the control room was mounting steadily. We went deep and opened [moved away] from the cruiser's port side to about 4,000 yards. She was flanked by two destroyers.

'At about 1600 (2000 London time) we fired three Mk8 torpedoes at the *Belgrano*. The atmosphere was electric as the seconds ticked away: forty-three seconds after discharge we heard the first explosion, followed by two more – three hits from three weapons. The control room was in an uproar, thirty people shouting and cheering.

'The captain, at the attack periscope, was screaming out orders – 10 down, starboard 30, half ahead, 130 revs. Everyone was hysterical, stamping and cheering, and it became quiet only after two or three minutes. We went deep. Then, after about five minutes, there was a loud bang – a depth charge. Everyone

75

froze, but the skipper ordered shut off for counter attack and we took evasive measures, hurtling down to [deleted] feet. There was silence throughout the boat – suddenly it was no longer fun to be doing what we were. We were at the receiving end.'

Lieutenant Sethia of the submarine *Conqueror*,
quoted in the *Observer* 25 November 1984

The most bizarre element in the Murrell murder case is what connection there could possibly be between the killing of a seventy-nine-year-old rose-grower and Mrs Thatcher's decision to sink the Argentinian battleship *General Belgrano* during the Falklands War. It was not the incident but the subsequent cover-up which provided the mistake which would lead to her tragic death.

To see why, it is necessary to go very briefly through the events leading to the Falklands campaign and the decision to sink the *Belgrano*. When Mrs Thatcher took office she inherited the 'problem' of the Falkland Islands – what should be done about this remaining far-flung outpost of British sovereignty? In 1977 the Labour government had come to the conclusion that the best option was to negotiate a lease-back arrangement with the Argentinians, ceding sovereignty in exchange for a long lease and a commitment to ensure the rights of the islanders. At that time it was felt most of them would agree to such an arrangement. Negotiations continued during the first months of the Thatcher administration without much attention being paid to them, although the Argentinians were becoming increasingly restive as they pressed for the return of the Malvinas (the Argentinian name for the Falklands).

Junior Foreign Office Minister Nicholas Ridley was despatched to the South Atlantic on two occasions to look into the matter and finally, in November 1980, the Foreign Secretary, Lord Carrington, carefully broached the idea of lease-back to the Prime Minister. Her reaction was, he described later, 'thermonuclear'[1]. Nor was she alone in it. When the matter came before the House on 2 December 1980 patriots from

76

all sides stood up to demand that sovereignty be kept over a group of islands to which most of them had never given a second thought until that moment. 'There followed,' writes Sir Ian Gilmour, 'the silliest half hour I have ever heard in Parliament. The blimps of all parties rushed in . . . Did they ever reflect, one wonders, that their conduct might well have helped to cause the deaths of 255 brave British servicemen – one for every seven inhabitants of the Falkland Islands?'[2]

Nicholas Ridley, to give him credit, did his best to point out the logistical impracticality of trying to defend islands at the other side of the world, warning the House that the Argentinians were becoming increasingly annoyed at the lack of progress in the negotiations. He begged the House not to 'behave as if the problem did not exist'. His pleas fell on deaf ears.

Certainly the Argentinian regime was deeply unpleasant but there were many precedents for negotiating with nasty regimes. Indeed in a number of cases, like that of Chile, we actually sold arms to them. But the idea of 'giving up the Falklands' released emotions among MPs that would eventually turn into a floodtide of jingoistic euphoria in the general population unprecedented since 1914.

Yet at the same time the Treasury was demanding deep cuts in public expenditure. It was decided, therefore, as part of general defence savings, to remove the only British naval presence in the South Atlantic, HMS *Endurance*. It was a fatal decision. Not only did it remove an excellent intelligence-gathering source on the military intentions of the Argentinian government, it sent exactly the wrong signal – that Britain was abandoning its claim to the Falkland Islands.

As Shakespeare's Henry IV told Prince Hal, there is nothing like a foreign war for taking a people's minds off a deeply unpopular government, and in this case the axiom applied both in Argentina and Britain. Beset by raging inflation, hated and feared in equal proportion and condemned by the world for its policy of 'disappearance', the Argentine government, under

General Galtieri, decided to launch an assault to reclaim the Falkland Islands. Intelligence to this effect was promptly passed on by MI6 to the Joint Intelligence Committee in London, reinforced by a warning on 3 March 1982 from the British Ambassdor in Buenos Aires in an urgent telegram. According to the Franks Committee, which later investigated the run-up to the Falklands War, Mrs Thatcher scribbled on the telegram in her own handwriting, 'We must have contingency plans.'[3]

On 19 March the *Endurance*, which was in Port Stanley, the capital of the Falklands, was ordered to sail for the island of South Georgia, taking with it a contingent of twenty-two marines, to look into a report that Argentinian scrap-metal workers had landed to remove the remains of an old whaling station. The captain of the *Endurance*, Nick Barker, derived a certain amount of wry amusement over the order since he had been told, when he had visited the Foreign Office the previous year to plead for *Endurance* to remain on station, that he was causing displeasure 'in high places'. But the 'scrap merchants' had been joined by a contingent of Argentinian marines under the command of Captain Astio Astiz, known popularly as 'el Rubio' and 'the Butcher of Cordoba' for his role in the junta's dirty war. The Argentinians, having raised their flag and laid some mines, returned to their ship and anchored just outside territorial waters. The British marines were ordered to stay on board while *Endurance* patrolled along the South Georgia coast.

So the countdown to the Falklands War began. The true position with regard to South Georgia was known to the government by 19 March but the pretence was kept up that the landing on South Georgia consisted only of half-a-dozen scrap-metal merchants. Meanwhile intelligence reports of preparations for the invasion of both South Georgia and the Falklands continued in a steady stream with the Prime Minister being fully informed. Yet she was to say in her statement to the House of Commons on 31 March 1982 that the invasion of the Falklands had come 'entirely out of the blue'.[4]

Within days Lord Carrington had resigned and the decision to despatch a Task Force to the South Atlantic had been taken. Mrs Thatcher's popularity shot up, as did that of her rival, and frantic international diplomatic activity began to try and prevent an all-out war. The chief emissary in the attempt was the American Secretary of State Al Haig who acted as go-between for the parties involved. Events moved swiftly. Britain announced an 'exclusion zone' for naval vessels in a wide area of the South Atlantic as the Task Force steamed south; meanwhile President Belaunde of Peru had come up with a possible peace plan, in the shape of a draft treaty drawn up with the assistance of Haig, whose own poposals had been rejected by the Argentinians.

Many words have been written arguing as to whether or not Mrs Thatcher's decision to sink the *General Belgrano* was deliberately designed to scupper the Peruvian peace plan. Whatever the real truth of the matter, and there are cogent arguments on both sides, the result was the same. The conflict continued, a conflict greeted with rapture by a population which sat in front of its television screens watching with tears in its eyes as the Task Force set out for the South Atlantic. Given that tide of popular feeling, it is possible to agree with what Alan Clark noted in his published diaries when considering the aftermath of that controversial decision, that most people could not have cared less if the *Belgrano* had been sunk while tied up safely in port.

By 30 April, as the Task Force approached the Falklands, Britain's Total Exclusion Zone officially came into force. The previous day the *General Belgrano* and her two destroyer escorts had left the port of Ushuaia. An ancient American battleship which had survived Pearl Harbour and later been sold to the Argentinians, she was thought of as little better than a floating museum and at no time did she ever carry Exocet missiles. Her orders were to sail east on a bearing of 110 and to avoid the Exclusion Zone. On 30 April the nuclear submarine, HMS *Conqueror* was ordered first to find, then monitor, the movements of the *Belgrano* and her escorts.

May 1 saw sporadic British attacks on Argentinian positions at the same time as efforts were being made to implement the Belaunde peace plan. The new Foreign Secretary, Francis Pym, flew to Washington, where he gave a press conference saying that these attacks had been designed to concentrate the minds of the Argentinians in the search for a peaceful solution. Meanwhile the *Belgrano* steamed steadily on.

The following day Rear-Admiral John Woodward asked for a change in the Rules of Engagement to enable him to sink the *Belgrano*. His reason, he said some months later, was that he feared that his force might be caught in a pincer movement between it and the aircraft carrier *25 de Mayo*. The situation was discussed at Naval Intelligence Headquarters at Northwood in Middlesex during a regular meeting of Chiefs of Staff attended by the Chief of Defence Staff, Admiral Sir Terence Lewin. Lewin later said he did not know of Woodward's request until that meeting.

Lewin then left for Chequers and a meeting with the Prime Minister, the content of which has never been revealed. Clive Ponting in his book *The Right to Know* suggests Lewin wanted permission for an all-out sinking of Argentinian vessels, not just the *Belgrano*.[5] Ponting was the senior civil servant at the Ministry of Defence who would later stand trial for leaking information to Labour M.P. Tam Dalyell. There is no doubt that at the time the Prime Minister had no reservations about ordering the attack, for the following Christmas, while taking a party which included composer Andrew Lloyd Webber around Chequers, she pointed to a chair with the words, 'This is the chair I sat in when I decided to sink the *Belgrano*.' The change in the Rules of Engagement was signalled to the *Conqueror* at 1330 hours but it was another six and a half hours before the fatal torpedoes were launched. At 1500, *Conqueror* signalled Northwood giving the *Belgrano*'s position, a signal which proved beyond all possible doubt that she had changed course and was sailing away from the Task Force and back towards the Argentinian mainland. There was clearly no threat. Various explanations have been given for the delay between the order and its implementation, one of which is that the captain of the *Conqueror* could not understand why the *Belgrano* still had to be sunk. Certainly signals continued to pass back and forth between the submarine and Northwood. At approximately 2000 London time *Conqueror* sank the *Belgrano* with the loss of 368 Argentinian lives.

News of the sinking reached Northwood on 2 May. As Monday the 3rd was a Bank Holiday it was not discussed in the House of Commons until the afternoon of 4 May, when Mrs Thatcher told MPs, in answer to a question from Michael Foot, that John Nott would be making a full statement on the incident. The *Belgrano*, she said, had carried very heavy armaments and had been such a threat to the Task Froce that an urgent decision was required: 'Had we left it any later it would have been too late and I might have had to come to the House with the news that some of our ships had been sunk.'[6]

Half an hour later Defence Minister John Nott rose and made the main statement in which he said on 2 May at 2000 London time, 'one of our submarines detected the Argentine cruiser, *General Belgrano*, escorted by two destroyers. This heavily armed surface-attack group was close to the Total Exclusion Zone and closing on elements of our Task Force, which was only hours away. We knew that the cruiser itself had substantial fire power, provided by fifteen six-inch guns with a range of thirteen miles, and Seacat anti-aircraft missiles. Together with its escorting destroyers, which we believe were equipped with Exocet anti-ship missiles with a range of more than twenty miles, the threat to the Task Force was such that the Task Force commander could ignore it only at his peril. The House will know that the attack by our submarine involved the capital ship only and not its escorting destroyers, so they should have been able to go to the assistance of the damaged cruiser. We do not know whether they did so, but, in doing so, they would not have been engaged.'[7]

The statement, approved by Mrs Thatcher, contained many

inaccuracies as subsequent events were to prove, but it was the story to which she would stick through thick and thin for the next two years. The *Belgrano* was not detected at 2000 London time on 2 May but over forty-eight hours previously. It was not 'closing on elements of our Task Force', but sailing away, and had been doing so for eleven hours. The attack did involve the escorting destroyers, one of which had been hit by a torpedo which failed to explode. Had they tried to pick up survivors, they might well have been sunk, as the orders countermanding such a possibility were not issued until the 4 May. The economy with the truth the Prime Minister exhibited over the sinking of the *Belgrano* threw a shadow which was to have an enduring impact on her reputation until the end of her term of office; yet ten years later, in her memoirs *The Downing Street Years*, she repeated the long since discredited story that the *Belgrano* had posed a threat and seemed utterly bewildered by the subsequent controversy. She also made clear her irritation at Haig's efforts to seek a negotiated settlement as she saw a war as a way to reverse the country's defeatist 'Suez Syndrome'. For Margaret Thatcher the aftermath of the *Belgrano* incident was largely an embarrassment. For Hilda Murrell it was fatal.

It will be apparent from the above that all the crucial signals connected with the setting up of the Total Exclusion Zone, the Rules of Engagement and the orders and queries passing back and forth to the *Conqueror* and ships sailing with the Task Force must have been dealt with by Naval Intelligence at Northwood.

But there had always been those who had been less than enthusiastic about the Falklands campaign and who felt that it had left behind many unanswered questions. From well before the 1983 election campaign, Tam Dalyell, Labour MP for Linlithgow, had been harrying the government on a range of Falklands issues, including that of the sinking of the *Belgrano*, a decision which he certainly believed had been taken to destroy a negotiated settlement. His persistent efforts were greeted largely with derision on the Conservative benches and with indifference on his own, at least at first. But as time went on the questions he asked about the *Belgrano* incident became increasingly detailed and it was obvious he had a source, or sources, of information sufficiently specific for him to be able to give the House particulars of the battleship's course; he maintained that she could not possibly have posed a threat to the Task Force as she had been steering west-north-west, in the opposite direction. The government response was that this was entirely untrue.

By the time the 1983 election campaign began in earnest, the attitude of most television and radio interviewers when dealing with the Prime Minister had degenerated into what can only be described as a sycophantic cringe, a posture they would continue to adopt for a further six years. The practice was that Mrs Thatcher should choose her interviewer and care would be taken to ensure she knew exactly what she would be asked and that the interviewer was aware which subjects must not be discussed. However, during the cut and thrust of the campaign something slipped when, on 24 May, she appeared on BBC Television's *Nationwide*, a programme which allowed ordinary members of the public to phone in with questions.

Among the questioners was a Mrs Diana Gould from Bristol with a question about the sinking of the *Belgrano*. Mrs Thatcher responded with the mantra that she and her government had been repeating for twelve months, that the battleship had been closing in on the Task Force and posed a threat. But, unlike the professional interviewers, Mrs Gould stoutly refused to be put off and asked the Prime Minister why it had been necessary to sink the ship when it was sailing away from the Falklands.

At first Mrs Thatcher sought to deflect her interrogator but, convinced by now that the Prime Minister was not telling the truth, Mrs Gould kept going until finally Mrs Thatcher, obviously losing her temper, barked out the now notorious reply 'but it was *not* sailing away from the Falklands!', and closed the subject. Mrs Gould had succeeded where professional journalists had failed. Neither she nor Tam Dalyell merits an entry in *The Downing Street Years*.

The rest, as they say, is history. Mrs Thatcher swept back to power with a huge majority on a tidal wave of triumphalism because of the Falklands War. She, who had been recorded in the opinion polls as the most unpopular Prime Minister ever, could do no wrong: she had shown Johnny Gaucho that the Brits could still teach him a thing or two. That men had died and, in the case of the *Galahad*, had suffered terrible injuries, was sad but it had been a famous victory.

Her election victory did not, however, deflect Tam Dalyell from his quest for the truth, a quest which was causing no little embarrassment to his own Front Bench, who were keen not to appear in any way unpatriotic. But insults and ridicule alike rolled off his back and his information became more and more precise.

At least some of his information came directly from *Conqueror* herself and Lieutenant Sethia was not the only one who had served on the submarine who was horrified at the lies surrounding the *Belgrano* affair. If, as most of the crew thought, the decision had been the right one, even if the battleship had been sailing away, then why was there any need for such an enormous cover-up? Other information, therefore, including details of signals, was added to Sethia's diary, the whole lot was then copied and passed along a chain through the hands of a publisher (who has since died) and finally, through a further intemediary, to Tam Dalyell.[8] It must be emphasized here that he has never revealed his sources either to myself or to anyone else. Meanwhile, two defence experts, Arthur Gavshon and Desmond Rice, were working on a book to be published early in 1984 which would contain all known information from every possible source.

While government Ministers continued to rubbish Dalyell to enthusiastic cheers from their supporters every time he raised the matter in the House, behind the scenes they were becoming increasingly uneasy as more and more information leaked out.

There also seems to have been a deliberate attempt at misinformation, for a number of newspapers carried stories to the effect that the log of the *Conqueror* – which would prove once and for all who was telling the truth – had 'gone missing'. Later the *Daily Mail* was to lay this at Sethia's door, leading to a libel action which cost them £260,000 and costs. The story must have been deliberately circulated to sympathetic journalists as the government were perfectly well aware what had happened to the log and where it was: in Washington.

Conqueror's prime task before the outbreak of the Falklands conflict had been to act as a spy ship, primarily for the Americans. One of its duties had been to monitor special sounding equipment used to follow the movements of Soviet warships. It was for this reason that Washington wanted to see the log; the sinking of the *Belgrano* was peripheral as the US administration was well aware of the truth of the matter from information provided by the CIA.[9]

Various members of the crew of *Conqueror* were hauled in for interrogation at Naval Intelligence headquarters at Northwood and one at least felt concerned enough to turn up for his hearing in civvies so that he could not find himself facing a court martial.

By December 1983 Dalyell's questioning was being taken sufficiently seriously for a special inquiry to be set up under the auspices of Cabinet Secretary Sir Robert Armstrong with a brief to investigate the leaks with extreme urgency. One possibility under consideration was that the source might be a disaffected operative at GCHQ Cheltenham. There was ongoing unrest among civil servants at the communications and intelligence centre following the government's announcement that it was to ban trade unions there. Various personnel were therefore to be 'checked out' by the security services and the results notified to Sir Robert.

Inquiries proved unsuccessful and 1984 dawned with Tam

Dalyell still persisting with his embarrassing questions, while behind the scenes frantic top-level meetings were being held to discuss the flow of information and whether or not the cover-up should be maintained. During the first week in March a senior civil servant, Clive Ponting, became Head of DS5, one of the divisions within the Ministry of Defence responsible for controlling military operations. His brief was to have been the monitoring of the Iran-Iraq war but instead he found himself 'dealing with the political consequences of a decision taken two years earlier . . .'

Two weeks later he was in Michael Heseltine's office as a discussion raged around him as to whether or not the truth should officially be told. Heseltine was heard around Westminster saying, 'I want to be quite sure there is not a Watergate in this somewhere!' Ponting was given the job of collecting all the relevant information on the *Belgrano* incident and at a 'frantic' pace records from archives and papers from other divisions of the MoD were read and processed, also detailed information held at Northwood, including highly classified material, was passed on and collated so that a decision could be taken. The document produced by Ponting as a précis of all the information was considered so explosive that it became known as 'the Crown Jewels'.

On 6 March Michael Heseltine received a letter from Labour's Defence Spokesman Denzil Davies. It had taken Labour's Shadow Cabinet a long time to get behind Tam Dalyell, but they had finally roused themselves with the publication of the Gavshon and Rice book and were asking for detailed replies to questions raised by it.

On 19 March 1984 Heseltine received a far more worrying letter. It was from Dalyell himself and it asked nineteen detailed questions about the *Belgrano* sinking. It was clear, writes Ponting in *The Right to Know*, 'that Dalyell had had access to some very accurate information. The Government had never acknowledged the detailed sequence of events over the period 30 April to 2 May 1982, yet Dalyell obviously knew exactly what they were.' Neither then, nor at any other time, has Dalyell ever revealed the sources of his information.

March 19 is a crucial date, for it was then that one of the sources told Dalyell of 'a tremendous flap in Downing Street', during which the order was given that the source or sources must be found at all costs.

Armstrong's inquiry had drawn a blank. Various possibilities were considered. Could it be that copies of 'raw signals' to and from *Conqueror*, the originals of which were supposed to have been destroyed at the end of hostilities on government orders, had come into Tam Dalyell's hands? Further inquiries were made at Northwood, where it was discovered that the first person to resign from Naval Intelligence at the end of the Falklands campaign had been a Commander Robert Green. As Dalyell was later to tell the House on 20 December 1984, 'He came under a cloud of suspicion, wrongly to the best of my knowledge . . .'

It needs emphasising here that no one who has researched Hilda Murrell's murder and the events surrounding it considers for one moment that Robert Green was a source of leaked information. Anyone who met him in the months after Hilda's death would have been aware that he was the very model of a retired naval man with deeply held conventional views. Whatever doubts he might have had during the run-up to the Falklands campaign, he believed it was right to send the Task Force and at no time has he criticised the decision to sink the *Belgrano*. On top of that, as he told me himself, even if he had had such a betrayal of trust in mind, the last thing he would have done would have been to put a much-loved close relative at risk by using her as recipient for stolen documents. To this day he vows that Hilda's death has nothing whatsoever to do with his work for Naval Intelligence.[10]

However, as Green had had to have extensive positive vetting because of the nature of his work, he must have been checked out once again. When people work in such sensitive areas and are vetted in this way, their friends and family go on file too.

Parents, siblings, wives, emotional involvements and close friends, all come under scrutiny. So naturally, when Green's record came up on screen, it would be noted that his parents were dead and that the closest relative with whom he had regular contact was his aunt, one Hilda Murrell, a rose-grower from Shrewsbury.

If any further evidence is needed for his being an unlikely candidate for leaking documents, then it can be found in his naval record at the time he left the navy in which he is particularly praised for liaison work with MI5 and MI6. 'He has been particularly good', it reads, 'in strengthening the many contacts with outside intelligence agencies and has earned their respect to a greater degree than SO[I]s [Senior Officers, Intelligence] have done for many years.'

It may be that it was quite fortuitous, that someone in the security services felt the name rang a bell, but it is more likely that there was a cross reference by Hilda's name on Green's file, to further information held elsewhere, most likely on a file maintained by MI5. It would not take long for a connection to be made which would lead to disaster. A naval officer who had left the service because he was disillusioned with the career prospects and who had had access to vital information regarding the sinking of the *Belgrano* had an aunt who was well-known for 'subversive' anti-nuclear activity and as an outspoken critic of government policy. It was something that had to be looked into.

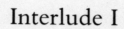

Interlude I

Chapter 8

Inquest

The feeling of unease over the progress of the investigation into Hilda's death and the number of unanswered questions it raised continued to grow steadily during the summer and into the autumn of 1984, and indeed carried over into 1985. As well as the contradictory police statements regarding the reporting of Hilda's abandoned car and Ian Scott's assertion that there was no body in the copse at the time he was there, there were a number of other anomalies. Although the police had continually appealed for witnesses, a number of those who had come forward had either, like Constance Purcer, had difficulty in persuading the police to hear what they had to say or had simply found themselves ignored. Among those who had expected to be contacted but were not was Hilda's young friend Catriona Guthrie, whose current boyfriend had family connections with the intelligence services. It was nine years before that oversight was rectified.

Then there is the matter of Hilda's telephones at her Shrewsbury house and at the Shack in North Wales, both apparently and coincidentally out of order. With regard to the former, the police have always maintained that the wires had been brutally ripped out of their socket and left hanging.[1] There are at least two witnesses who say otherwise.

To start with, there is the evidence of Brian George when he first entered Ravenscroft on the morning Hilda's body was discovered. He found the appearance of the telephone so odd that he fetched his daughter over to draw a picture of it. The junction box was screwed in place but the wires to the receiver had been removed. They had not been 'torn' or yanked out, they were only an inch or so away and each still retained its small hook. The telephone itself was across the handset at an angle.

Brian George has recently made a statement maintaining that he has been under pressure from West Mercia Police to change his story as to the appearance of the telephone.

Indeed, early in 1985, an informed source within British Telecom told both myself[2] and the *Evening Standard*[3] that the telephone had indeed been expertly dealt with, or at least put out of action by someone who knew what he was doing. The junction box appeared to have been unscrewed and just one of the wires inside the incoming cord (the green one) had been cut. The box was then screwed back on and there were no loose incoming wires. The result would be that to all intents and purposes the line was dead, but that anyone telephoning in would apparently hear the telephone ringing out as if there was no reply. In actual fact the sound heard by any caller would occur at the exchange, for the green wire governs the bell on the individual telephone set.

The source went further. All telephones, at least at that time, had a card on file with British Telecom to record any maintenance work carried out, but the card for Hilda's number on file at the British Telecom depot at Ditherington, Shrewsbury, carried no reference either to the damage caused by the supposed burglary or to the subsequent investigation of the telephone line. This ties in with the suggestion that her telephone had been tapped, as when that is the case any faults arising are repaired by special, not routine, engineers.

In the early months of 1985 two television programmes were

devoted to the Murrell murder, Granada's *World in Action* on 4 March and a second BBC *Crimewatch* on 14 March. Stuart Prebble, the Granada producer, asked the police if he could photograph the phone connection at Hilda's house to show how the wires had been ripped from the wall; his request was refused on the grounds that the manner of disconnection was confidential.[4]

It was, therefore, with some surprise that Stuart Prebble watched *Crimewatch*, only to see what was claimed to be a police video proving that the wires had been ripped out of the wall. In fact what was shown was a picture of some telephone wires hanging loose from a socket, a shot which could have been taken anywhere, followed by one of a police officer holding a length of broken telephone cable.

Regarding the telephone at the Shack, the Home Office Minister Giles Shaw, in reply to a question in the Commons from Tam Dalyell, claimed that it had been out of order due to storm damage. Dalyell duly checked the weather records, only to find that there had been no storm in the Llanymynech area throughout February or March 1984.[5] Subsequent questioning by Gerald Kaufman MP elicited from the then Home Secretary, Leon Brittan, that no fault had been found with the telephone at the Shack, but that a capacitator had failed at the telephone exchange due to storm damage. He admitted, however, that 'it does not appear that the lines of any other subscribers were affected in a similar way. This particular fault is most commonly known to occur as a result of lightning and storm damage; moreover it can happen that the defect does not become evident for a number of months. . . In the view of the engineer who maintains the records, lightning is not uncommon at any time of year in the Welsh border region.' He concluded by saying that there was 'no evidence of human interference in its operation'.[6]

So much for the telephone.

But as well as the abandoned car and the two telephones, there was also the question of why police statements had differed so substantially as to the state of Hilda's house that Saturday morning. First it was said to have been ransacked, then methodically and systematically searched.[7] As to the conflicting statements as to whether or not Hilda had actually been sexually assaulted, this could be put down to the fact that the police had not wanted to distress the family further by giving details of what was obviously a perverted act.

But there has never been any adequate explanation of the extraordinary circumstance in which the police constable first on the scene claims he spent two hours thoroughly searching the house without discovering whether or not Hilda was actually there or finding anything amiss, in spite of an open door, drawn curtains and lights blazing, a pile of unopened post, a rolled up wet sheet on the floor, a newly damaged banister rail and several handbags standing on a table.

It is now necessary to make a brief reference to my own involvement in this story. In the late summer of 1984 I was contacted by a friend of Hilda Murrell who knew that I had been involved in a number of stories requiring investigation. At the time I was trying to change direction professionally and I have to admit firstly that I did not initially believe there was anything sinister about Hilda Murrell's death – all investigative journalists are only too used to receiving pleas for help from friends and relatives of those alleged to have been victims of some kind of conspiracy – and secondly, to be frank, even if there was I had no desire as a freelance to become involved.

However, having read reports of the case, visited the area and spoken to a number of people, I decided to see what Robert Green had to say. I left his house after the first visit substantially shaken, having learned something of the part he had played during the Falklands campaign. By this time, convinced that something was very wrong and concerned that I was involved for the first time in such a story without the back-up of a newspaper, I decided to contact Tam Dalyell about the possibility of a connection with the sinking of the *Belgrano*.

His response was immediate and from then on we were in constant touch which, in view of the surveillance to which I later found myself subjected, was something of a comfort.

By the end of October 1984 I felt I had, at the very least, sufficient information to publish the story so far as I knew it and see if there was any reaction. My first port of call was the *Guardian*, with which I had had a long relationship, but the editor to whom I put the idea, along with its provenance, turned it down as being insufficiently strong to merit the trouble it might cause. This was not long after the young civil servant Sarah Tisdall had been sent to gaol for leaking a document to the paper which they had given to the relevant authorities when requested to do so.

Next on the list was the *New Statesman*, to which, at that time, I was a regular contributor; the story was finally broken on 9 November under the heading 'The Death of Miss Murrell'. With hindsight, and having accumulated so much more information, I acknowledge that there were some inaccuracies: the basic information on the finding of the body and the consequent trail of strange events is nevertheless substantially correct, although I had left the *Belgrano* connection deliberately vague at the express request of Robert Green.

On 5 December the inquest into the death of Hilda Murrell was finally held at Shrewsbury Magistrates' Court. It was here that Home Office Pathologist Dr Peter Acland described the injuries to the body detailed earlier. Following on from this statement, and in answer to questions from the Coroner, Dr Acland agreed that there was some evidence that the dead woman might have been crawling at some stage and that he could not be totally sure that she had died on the exact spot where she was found: 'She could have died up to a hundred yards away . . .' Questioned as to the time of death, he judged that it was between five and ten hours after she had been abandoned.

Dr Acland also referred to the second post mortem in order to inform the inquest that this had not been his decision, but that the second pathologist, a Dr Gower, had 'entirely agreed with all my findings and conclusions' and 'no new evidence came to light as a result of this'. It was then that he agreed that it was possible, but unlikely, that the body had been moved after death.[8]

The Coroner then told the inquest that it was usual practice to retain the body of a murder victim so that when a person was charged they could have their own post mortem carried out. However in this particular case he had been advised that the 'natural processes were reaching a stage when it would shortly thereafter be quite impractical for a second post mortem to be subsequently carried out if somebody was charged. Advice was taken and we were advised to have a second post mortem so that that second post mortem could be made available to the defence if and when someone was charged.'[9]

The second witness was Detective Chief Superintendent David John Cole, who began by saying that while he was prepared to disclose as much evidence as possible to assist the inquest he was not prepared to disclose it all. 'This is in no way an attempt to conceal anything, but I must be in a position to put evidence to a suspect which has not been previously released so that the accuracy of anything a suspect tells me may be tested.'

He then covered the discovery of the body and subsequent police investigation, pointing out his difficulties, not least of which was the fact that Hilda had been such a private person and that it was hard, therefore, to build up a picture of the pattern of her life. However, 'I believe that, on returning to her home, Miss Murrell either disturbed an intruder in her premises or was followed into her house by the offender. There is no evidence of forced entry.'

With regard to Ian Scott's statement, Cole said that the police were aware that he had been in the Moat Wood at approximately 3.30 p.m. on 22 March 1984 and that he had claimed that he 'did not see Miss Murrell's body. This has been carefully considered and researched. He may be mistaken. The body was in a slight hollow and dressed in clothing which matched the undergrowth.'

Sixty-nine witnesses to the sighting of a white Renault being driven erratically out of Shrewsbury had been traced and interviewed, and artists' impressions issued of 'the alleged offender', the running man. A reconstruction of the journey of the running man had brought in a further forty-nine witness statements. The investigation had been a thorough and wide-ranging one. Some 3,590 persons had been nominated as potential suspects and all had been researched by both 'local and national intelligence agencies'. As a result, a total of 962 persons had been 'processesed' and 491 of these interviewed.

As certain newspapers had suggested that Miss Murrell's death was connected with her anti-nuclear activities, this had been given careful consideration and looked into, but the small team of officers specifically assigned to this task had failed to find any evidence connecting Miss Murrell's Sizewell B project to her death. 'I am still left with the inescapable conclusion that this was an offence of burglary, and the offender was after, in the main, cash. There is evidence contained within my incident room which leads to that conclusion.'

He summed up, 'The depth of the inquiry is revealed by the following figures which are from the period 21.3.84 to 30.11.84 when they were updated last:

'We have pursued 4,404 lines of inquiry.

'We have pursued 1,361 messages from members of the public attempting to give us information on this matter.

'My officers have recorded 2,162 statements from potential witnesses.

'They have submitted to me for consideration 101 reports in connection with various matters throughout the inquiry.

'The major incident room records now total individual indices of 55,086 records.

'We have visited 4,800 houses during house-to-house inquiries in an attempt to obtain information.

'We have interviewed 11,900 residents of Shrewsbury and have set up road checks and checked 1,570 vehicles.'[10]

It can be noted that in this massive welter of statistics there is no mention of any inquiry being made into the surveillance activities of the various investigation bureaux monitoring Sizewell objectors. This was because West Mercia Police apparently did not know of their existence, even though they had taken advice, according to Cole, from, among others, 'national and local intelligence agencies'.

After hearing the evidence of Dr Acland and Chief Superintendent Cole, the Coroner formally found that Hilda had died on either 21 or 22 March 1984 at Hunkington from a combination of hypothermia and wounds to the abdomen.

'The only verdict that I can record in such a case is that the deceased was killed unlawfully.'

PART III

Politics II

Chapter 9

The Matter Before the House

It was almost exactly a month after Hilda's death that Clive Ponting sent Tam Dalyell his first note. Appalled by the sheer scale and magnitude of the *Belgrano* cover-up after all the work he had put into 'the Crown Jewels', Ponting wrestled with his years of training as a civil servant and took his decision. The note, unsigned, gave Tam the answers to three of the questions he had asked in Parliament on 19 March, those questions which had caused such a manic reaction at 10 Downing Street. Ponting's view was that the answers to them were technically unclassified under normal circumstances.[1]

He also gave the junior Defence Minister, John Stanley, the same answers and suggested he gave them to Tam, but Stanley refused. The cover-up was to continue with its protagonists wading into ever deeper water, from deliberate attempts to mislead to a blanket refusal to answer any questions at all. John Stanley, in particular, absolutely adored the Prime Minister, telling Ponting, 'Margaret is too good for this country. The country does not deserve someone so outstanding. She is the greatest leader this country has been privileged to have this century, and that includes Winston Churchill.' His loyalty was absolute.

Ponting continued to urge both Stanley and Michael Heseltine to answer Dalyell's questions and put the whole matter straight, but his advice was ignored. Stanley told Heseltine he would have no difficulty in claiming information was classified when it was not and proposed sending a response to the House of Commons Select Committee set up to look into the future of the Falklands which would fudge the issue of the *Belgrano* and avoid any detailed answers to questions by offering only a 'general narrative'. Detailed information, they would be told, would 'be almost incomprehensible to laymen'.[2]

Ponting was faced with a stark choice. 'Ministers were now involved in blocking an inquiry by a Select Committee which had the right to inquire and get truthful answers. Ministers were also going to provide a misleading memorandum that would at best be "consistent with previous statements" and which had the clear purpose of blocking any further enquiries.' So, this high-flying civil servant with an impeccable career record put some crucial documents in an envelope and, on 16 July 1984, sent them to Tam Dalyell. Ten days later they were back inside the Ministry of Defence and a frantic search was on to find the mole. Ponting was arrested late on the evening of 16 August and brought before a special Magistrates' Court at the Old Bailey on Saturday 18 August charged with breaking the Official Secrets Act.

It is unlikely that much thought was given at this time to the death of a Shrewsbury rose-grower, although the intelligence services must have been aware that Dalyell had had top quality information long before the first contact with Ponting. They must also have known for months that nothing had been found in Hilda's house and that Robert Green had not passed on classified information to his aunt. I understand that the *New Statesman* piece of 9 November did cause some concern, but it was thought best to let the whole thing die down. After all, the inquest on Hilda Murrell was shortly to go ahead and that would be that, the end of the matter.

★   ★   ★

On 18 December Tam Dalyell learned that he had drawn a high place in the lottery of speakers in the Consolidated Fund Bill. This is one of Westminster's ancient rites which takes place before parliamentary breaks and in which MPs can raise any matter of interest to them, even if there are only a handful of people in the Chamber to listen. It often drags on into the night and usually passes without anyone outside Westminster knowing that it has taken place. Not this time, however.

Shortly beforehand, Tam had learned from his sources (not Ponting, who was now awaiting trial), that there had indeed been a semi-official break-in at the home of Hilda Murrell. The reason the source had not come forward earlier was the extreme concern felt throughout the civil service over the fate of Clive Ponting. Put brutally, Ponting's colleagues did not want to find themselves standing beside him in the dock.

What Tam was told was that the operation had not been organised at a very high level. There had been no intention of harming Hilda, but it had been decided to search her house to see if she had any copies of documents or raw signals. It is likely that she had first become suspect following the meeting in December 1993 when Sir Robert Armstrong had been asked to chair the special committee looking into the *Belgrano* case, then it was the furore of 19 March 1984 which was finally to seal her fate. As will be shown later, however much he may have been criticised since, Tam's early information was to prove remarkably accurate.

There were at least two intruders and Hilda had come home unexpectedly and disturbed them. She was injured, then taken away, dumped and left to die.

Early in the evening of 19 December Paddy Ashdown, who had been very sympathetic to Robert Green, rang him and read him the lengthy statement Tam intended making when called to speak. Tam meanwhile contacted me. We were on the point of leaving on the night train for London to visit my parents in France and Tam and I agreed we should speak again when I reached Paddington.

At 3.51 a.m. precisely, in the early hours of 20 December, Tam rose to address a sleepy House. He began by stating that his interest had been aroused by the 9 November *New Statesman* piece and went on to give MPs the bare bones of the murder. Most of them had never heard of Hilda Murrell or her death. He then explained the *Belgrano* connection, emphasising that the suspicions surrounding any leak of information from Green to his aunt were entirely unfounded, for Green 'to the best of my extensive knowledge . . . has behaved absolutely properly as a naval officer loyal to the navy in not talking about information gleaned when in the navy'.

He also praised the courtesy of the police but expressed surprise that Special Branch had been called in. He drew attention to the forensic reports and listed some of the anomalies in the events surrounding Hilda's death. He brought up the question of the abandoned car, the 'ransacking' of a house which it was later admitted had not been ransacked, the state of the telephones, the supposed forced entry of Hilda's house by West Mercia Police even though witnesses had seen them walk in through the door and the doubt as to whether or not Hilda had indeed been the victim of a sexual assault.

A small number of MPs had slumbered on through the early part of Tam's speech but gradually, as rumours got around that Dalyell, crazy though he might be, was to make some remarkable allegations against the intelligence services, more members made their way to the Chamber.

The MPs began to wake up. Potential witnesses, Tam claimed, had been made to feel foolish. 'Does a police force which, I am told, has a good reputation for efficiency normally act like that or was it told on high authority to act in such an uncharacteristically slapdash way? Why did the police behave out of character? Ministers should tell us. I am told by more than one of the people interviewed by the police that they instinctively felt that the police officers knew jolly well that their time was being wasted and that they were having to go through the motions of a large-scale investigation for cosmetic reasons.'

Hilda Murrell in one of her many hats.

Hilda's house, 'Ravenscroft'.

Hilda's Renault 5 as it was found on the verge of the lane at Hunkington.

Police checkpoint at Hunkington crossroads, 28 March 1984.

West Mercia police roadblock close to the scene of the crime, 26 March 1984

West Mercia police officers searching Hilda's garden, 28 March 1984.

Police reconstruction. Detective Constable Steve Larrie following the route used by 'the running man', 4 April 1984.

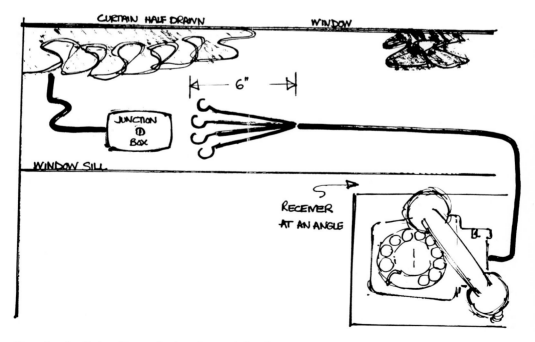

Drawing by Brian George's daughter of the disconnected phone on the morning of 24 March 1984.

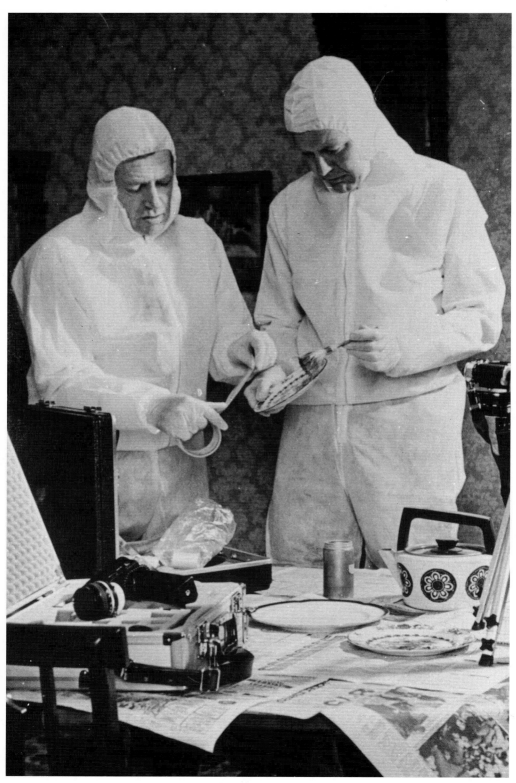

West Mercia forensic officers in 'scene-of-crime' suits, checking items in Hilda's house. Detective Sergeant David Peniton (left) is 'lifting' fingerprints on to tape for analysis.

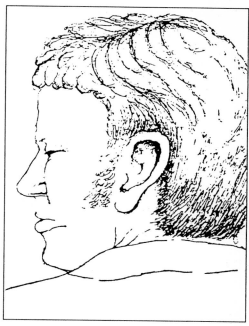

The two very different artist's impressions of the 'running man', released by West Mercia police in spring 1984.

Artist impression of the man wanted in connection with the murder of Sergeant John Speed released by West Yorkshire police. This later appeared in the *Yorkshire Post* on 27 January 1988 as David Griceworth (left).

The Argentine cruiser *General Belgrano* sinks in the South Atlantic, 1 May 1982.

Labour MP, Tam Dalyell.

He spoke of Hilda's fears that she was under surveillance. Tam, a known advocate of nuclear power, sought to discount any notion that the break-in had been authorised by the nuclear industry: 'Since more than twenty-two years ago, as a new Member of Parliament who was technologically minded and on the Public Accounts Committee, I was befriended by the late Sir Christopher Hinton, who later became Lord Hinton of Bankside OM – he was a great man and a great engineer and Chairman of the CEGB and Scottish generating boards – I cannot believe for one mini-second that Sir Walter Marshall, any of his colleagues, my friend Con Allday and others from the nuclear industry, would dream of authorising minions to search the house of a seventy-eight-year-old rose-grower who had elegantly expressed, but quite unoriginal, views on reactor choice and nuclear waste disposal.'

The inconsistencies in the conduct of the investigation, the unsatisfactory inquest which had raised more questions than it answered, all pointed 'away from a random murder and therefore away from the official explanation.'

He then spelled out why he had decided to broach the matter in that particular manner:

'I must candidly tell the Minister that in my previous twenty years in the House, I should have gone privately to the Home Secretary, regardless of party. I should have gone to Rab Butler, Henry Brooke, Frank Soskice, the Right Honourable Member for Hillhead [Roy Jenkins], my Right Honourable friend for Cardiff South and Penarth [Jim Callaghan] and my Right Honourable friend for Morley and Leeds South [Merlyn Rees] or, indeed, to Willie Whitelaw. I have known them all and had dealings with all of them. However, to some Ministers in the present government, to whom I have been the subject of ridicule and deception, I am not prepared to go. . . Least of all am I prepared to go to the present Home Secretary, who makes the type of speech about the miners that brings disgrace to the great office he holds.'

He then referred to his questions of 19 March and the

subsequent search for those leaking information 'pre Ponting'. So the operation was set up, including the disastrous search of Hilda's house which led to her death 'and the cover-up had to begin, because I am informed the searchers were men of the British intelligence.

'If Ministers cannot solemnly deny my belief about the participation of intelligence, on whose ministerial authority, if any, did the search of Miss Murrell's home take place? Was there clearance, or was this the intelligence services "doing their own thing"? Did they do it on political orders, and if so, on whose orders? Some of us have had increasing misgivings about the role of the intelligence services in this country – again I say this in the presence of my Honourable friend the Member for Bolsover [Dennis Skinner] – in connection with the miners' strike.'

There should be, he continued, a Select Committee of Privy Councillors to which all the intelligence services should be made accountable, but until that happened he would continue to ask questions and name people under the cover of parliamentary privilege.

'I ought to add that Commander Green was, I am told, the person who physically sent the signal to *Conqueror* that sank the *Belgrano*. I understand from his friends that he was also responsible for passing signals from *Endurance* which had shown beyond any reasonable doubt that an invasion of the Falklands was about to happen.'

He concluded, 'He considered the Falklands to be an unnecessary war, and the *Belgrano* sinking appalled him – albeit he adjudged it an unfortunate necessity – as it did some other senior officers of the senior service. He took early retirement after twenty years in the navy and left. From this Prime Minister and her colleagues he would come under suspicion. It is from the head of our security services that Parliament should be demanding an explanation, because of one thing I am certain – that there are persons in Westminster and Whitehall who know a great deal more about the violent death of Miss Hilda Murrell than they have so far been prepared to divulge.'

Tam then sat down. The time was 4.15 a.m.

He was followed by Paddy Ashdown. He had not, he said, been into the matter as fully as had Dalyell, but he had the highest respect for Robert Green and was deeply concerned at the serious allegations that had been made. He reminded the House how often in the past they had subjected Dalyell to ridicule only to discover that he had been in the right. 'In the absence of detailed answers to the detailed questions which the Honourable Member for Linlithgow has put, I believe that there is only one way forward: a full inquiry under a High Court judge.'

Ashdown went on at some length about the lack of accountability of the country's security services and how they should be under much more political control. 'At the very heart of this issue lies the system that we now refer to as "clearance". The intelligence services have to receive clearances at various appropriate levels, including – at the very highest level – that of the Prime Minister, before taking any action. I have no doubt that action such as that mentioned by the Honourable Member for Linlithgow would, under normal circumstances, have had to be approved at the very highest level.

'If what the Honourable Member says is true, it is inconceivable that it could have occurred under normal circumstances other than with agreement at the highest level. But if that did not happen, there must have been a significant breakdown in the way that our intelligence services are controlled. One must reach one or other of those conclusions if the Honourable Gentleman's thesis is supportable. Either a politician at a very high level was involved in taking the decision to allow such action to go ahead, or there must have been a very serious breakdown in the democratic and political accountability and control of our intelligence services.'

The response came from the Minister of State at the Home Office, Giles Shaw, an urbane and respected politician. He had been briefed on what was to come and led the House through the official version of the police investigation and the inquest without, however, providing satisfactory explanations for the anomalies Tam Dalyell had raised. He repeated the statistics given at the inquest by Chief Superintendent Cole on the number of people, telephone messages, statements and recorded items of information on file and computer. He expressed himself as being pleased that Tam had not blamed the nuclear industry for what had happened, or the fact that Hilda had been working on a paper for the Sizewell B Inquiry. He also made an interesting comment regarding the sheer size of the murder inquiry: 'If a police inquiry is continuing and its scale has reached these proportions, it may be considered odd, if there were a British security element involved in the investigation, or occasioning the crime for which the investigation has been set up, that it should continue without those involved being able to ensure that the police and security services are sharing common knowledge.' He assured the House that he had taken on board the comments of both the members for Linlithgow and Yeovil [Paddy Ashdown] and would give them a considered response.

Tam thanked him for taking the matter seriously. 'As long as there is a considered reply, whatever that reply may be – there will be no pressure from me to hurry the response. I certainly will not urge the Home Office to get on with the job and give a speedy reply. It can be a reply that takes weeks to obtain.'

Shaw then sat down. It was 4.53 a.m. and the House went on to debate a motion by Mr Robert B. Jones, MP for Hertfordshire West, on the financing of the BBC.

A little over an hour later travellers from the West Country arriving in Paddington off the overnight sleeper were greeted with an array of newspaper boards trumpeting the lead story in the final editions of the daily papers – that the murder of an anti-nuclear campaigner was being blamed on the security services. Hilda's face, under the brim of her floppy hat, stared out at the world from the front pages.

★　　★　　★

POLITICS II

On Monday 28 January 1985 Clive Ponting was brought to trial
charged under Section 2 of the Official Secrets Act. His solicitor
throughout had been a fine one, the late Brian Raymond, a man
with an impressive track record of fighting civil liberties causes;
he was to have personal experience of this during the course of
the trial, for it became apparent that both his and Ponting's
telephones were being tapped. First the junior QC for Ponting,
Jonathan Caplan, was approached by someone who claimed
to have heard that the defence team were complaining to the
judge about their telephone being tapped and so 'wondered
what reaction we had got'. This, says Ponting, was odd since
no such complaint had been made officially.

Next Brian Raymond was told by a journalist with intelligence sources, 'They say there's a flap on over there, because
your counsel's seeing the judge over his phone being bugged.
My sources say it's to do with something that blew up last
night.' The counsel had no such plans, but the journalist left
Raymond wondering how he had acquired the same piece of
information.[3]

The trial rolled on for two weeks under the eyes of the Attorney General, Sir Thomas Hetherington, who attended every
day. A full account of it and the detailed arguments on both
sides can be read in Ponting's own book, *The Right to Know*.
At the end of his final speech for the prosecution, Roy Amlot
QC launched into the theme which he believed had underpinned
the whole event: that the interests of the State and those of the
government of the day were synonymous and that the 'broader
interests of the State' meant that official information should be
kept secret. 'It's not just the law, it's good sense. It has applied
in this country for centuries.' It had therefore been essential, he
insisted, that the events surrounding the sinking of the *Belgrano*
be kept secret and those who had sought to break the law by
leaking such information, for whatever reason, undermined the
very process of government.

In reply Ponting's counsel, Bruce Laughland, explained yet
again what had prompted him to take such a course of action,

concluding, 'He was faced with an obligation to do his duty – in the true interests of the State – from which he did not shrink. If what he did was a crime, you know this could be a licence for Ministers to withhold information from the House of Commons with the tame acquiescence of their civil servants and so infringe your liberties.

'If what he did was a crime in English Law, you say so. But if it is, God help us – because no government will!'

The judge, Mr Justice McCowan, then embarked on a hostile summing up in which he made the notorious statement which enshrines, almost better than any other, the political climate of the time in which Hilda's murder took place:

'We have general elections in this country. The majority party in the House of Commons forms the government. If it loses majority support it ceases to do so, but for the time being it *is* the government and its policies *are* those of the State.' Hitler and Stalin would have heartily concurred, not to mention Saddam Hussein. Mr Justice McCowan left the jury in no doubt as to what he expected from them when they returned their verdict.

When they filed back into a packed court after their deliberations there was total silence. The clerk asked the foreman of the jury if they had reached a verdict. He replied that they had. It was the verdict of them all. 'Do you find the defendant Guilty or Not Guilty?' The foreman replied, 'Not Guilty.'

The people, at least on this occasion, had had enough of the interests of the State.

Chapter 10

Theories and Follow-Ups

Between Tam Dalyell's dramatic intervention in the Commons – leading to headlines such as that of the *Evening Standard*, 'MP's Amazing Murder Story' – and the Ponting verdict, the media had finally latched on to the Murrell story with mixed results. Theories abounded, from the sub Le Carré through Satanism and witchcraft to the 'it couldn't happen here' school of 'investigative' journalism.

One of the first off was *The Sunday Times*[1] in a piece largely designed to ridicule the notion that there could have been any official covert operation. Having described the break-in, attack on Hilda and her abduction, the paper gave Tam Dalyell rare praise from this particular quarter because he had stoutly exonerated the nuclear industry from any involvement.

It was admitted that Robert Green and his aunt might well have been suspects in the *Belgrano* leaks and Hilda might even have been under surveillance, but the likelihood was that it had indeed been a bungling opportunist (and perverted) burglar who had broken into Hilda's house coincidentally. However, it was conceded that at this point the security services, although not hitherto involved in the event, might well have needed to cover up the killer's tracks in order to draw attention away from their own surveillance: the cut telephone wires lent 'some support to this theory'. The wires might have been cut, for instance, to neutralise a listening device. This theory put the responsibility for the break-in and murder on the man the police were seeking as described by the FBI – a local unskilled loner – while that of covering up his traces lay at the door of the security services. *The Sunday Times* account admits that this still leaves some difficulties and quotes Detective Sergeant Barrie Mayne as saying, 'This doesn't follow the accepted pattern of burglaries; not in my experience as a policeman.'

However, the overall effect was to put the boot in to any suggestion that the break-in had, in any way, received official approval, although it is widely accepted that those used by the intelligence services on dodgy missions do so on the understanding that if they are caught they are on their own. They are officially known as 'temps'.

Five days later *Private Eye* advanced the theory that Hilda had become increasingly aware of being under surveillance and that when she had returned home unexpectedly and surprised an intruder or intruders she had reacted in a spirited fashion. Her assailants were well aware of her reputation; they knew she would have been prepared to make an enormous fuss over her discovery of people going through her private papers and would have had no compunction in going both to the authorities and to the media. She would also have been quite capable of recognising those involved, which might well have led to the discovery of who had authorised the break-in.

Therefore, after knocking her unconscious during the struggle, the intruders decided to dump her body well away from home in an attempt to avoid any questions being asked about why they had been there. The *Private Eye* theory was that this was why she had been abducted by one of the intruders, the other or others being left to tidy up the house and remove anything they wanted to take away. It is also suggested that Hilda came round while being driven to Hunkington and tried to force her abductor off the road, which would account for the descriptions of her car's erratic progress; also that it was she who threw a trail of belongings along the lane. The struggle forced the car off the road and on to the rock on which it was found. She was then hidden in a ditch while the driver returned to her house where efforts were made to make it look like a burglary by a kinky killer. The intruders returned on the evening of the following day, removed the body from the ditch and placed it carefully where it was found, grateful that the Shrewsbury police did not appear to have followed up the report of her abandoned car. At this stage, although they were later to change their minds, the *Private Eye* team pointed the finger at the nuclear police.

'I was Prime Murder Suspect' ran the headline in the *Evening Standard* of 8 January, detailing the experiences of the first suspect to break cover. His name was Robert James Higgins, and at the time of report he was awaiting trial for a string of burglaries. 'I know why the police thought it was me,' he told the *Standard*, 'but I didn't kill her.' Higgins had been picked out by a witness as the 'running man' and he was terrified that the murder would be pinned on him by a police force desperate to be seen to have succeeded in bringing in a murderer who fitted their theory. 'At one stage I was desperate,' said Higgins. When charged, he had pleaded guilty to two burglaries and a theft, asking for twenty other offences to be taken into consideration. 'They were under pressure to find someone for the murder and I just didn't have an alibi. I couldn't remember where I was on the day. I didn't even know about the murder until they told me.'

According to Higgins the police suspected him on three grounds: he could drive but had not passed his test and might therefore drive 'erratically'; he admitted burglaries on five homes and a school in the Shrewsbury area; he was picked out by a single witness as the running man. The last point was considered important as Higgins was a keen amateur runner and his diary for 21 March 1984 noted that he had run seven miles that day. It was also considered sinister that an anti–nuclear leaflet should have been found during the search of his flat. 'But I've been interested in nuclear weapons and the arms race for some time,' he claimed, 'it's something I think everyone should be interested in. It affects all of us and I think it's a good idea to know where you are.'

He was taken to Hilda's house, which he swore he did not recognise. 'Then, when I was picked out at the identity parade, I thought, Christ, that's it, they'll frame me. I couldn't remember where I was or what I'd done. They seemed sure it was me, but they didn't charge me.' His solicitor told Shrewsbury Magistrates that his client had been extensively interrogated and 'had been through hell'.

A day later Tam Dalyell received a letter[2] from a North London man who had read the piece in the *Standard*. In it he revealed that his sister-in-law's boyfriend had also been arrested in connection with Hilda's murder but, like Higgins, had not been charged. This suspect had been picked up in Ramsgate, after which the correspondent's home was extensively searched by Shrewsbury CID; they had taken various items 'and an affidavit they had no right to see. Despite our insistence that John was staying with us at the time, they proceeded to follow up every possible lead, travelling to Norwich and Dorset as well as around London and back to us once more.'

The police maintained throughout that the man was a prime suspect, although they had only hearsay evidence that he had been in Shrewsbury at the relevant time; but it is true that he had lived in the town some years previously and had a record of petty crime. He was finally released at the end of three days of interrogation after confessing to a minor theft. Throughout this time he was denied access to a solicitor and when the correspondent questioned the police as to the legality of this he was told 'he didn't want one'.

The next day, 10 January 1985, *The Times* carried an angry letter from the Home Office Pathologist, Dr Peter Acland. Having expressed his annoyance at the amount of speculation and controversy surrounding Hilda's death, some of which he felt had rubbed off on him, he wanted to put various matters on record. He himself had had nothing but co-operation from West Mercia Police and had never been denied any relevant information. 'I was not approached or influenced by any member of any Secret Service organisation. . . I do not believe either that any of the police officers were so influenced.' At the inquest, he continued, he had fully and frankly answered all questions and the reason for the second post mortem had been fully and satisfactorily explained.

'I am not sure what else I can do to satisfy the concern of the family. With the permission of the Coroner I am quite happy to discuss the case with any pathologist nominated by the family.

'I don't know who killed Miss Murrell, but I have a strong suspicion that some twopenny halfpenny thief is gloating over a pint of beer in a pub not many miles from Shrewsbury about all this media interest.'

On 16 January a Mr Peter Hurst informed the *Daily Mirror* that on the night of Tam Dalyell's speech his flat had been broken into. Hurst had recently retired from the navy and had been a close working colleague of Robert Green during the Falklands War; he was also, at that time, the only other officer who had served in such a capacity to have left the service. His flat, which was in the middle of a block in St Albans, was the only one to suffer that night and, although Hurst owned two television sets and an expensive hi-fi system, nothing at all was taken. However, his papers had been systematically gone through.

At first he had thought it an ordinary burglary 'but now I agree that it could just have some connection with the Hilda Murrell affair'. The police, however, immediately discounted this theory, even going so far as to say, before their investigation was completed, that it was coincidence, had nothing to do with Hilda's murder and that there had been several other burglaries in that part of St Albans about that time.

On 27 January Nick Davies in the *Observer*, assisted by Gary

Murray, came up with a story that the *Sunday Times* team of four reporters and a researcher appeared to have missed, i.e. that the Sizewell objectors really had been under surveillance. This shone the spotlight for the first time on the role of Zeus Securities in the surveillance of Sizewell objectors, which was admitted to by Peter Hamilton but, not surprisingly, with a strong disclaimer that it had had anything whatsoever to do with the Murrell murder.

Three days later Paul Foot in the *Daily Mirror* profiled Vic Norris/Adrian Hampson and his interesting past, pointing out that while no one was saying that he was directly involved in what happened in Shrewsbury, it was a chilling thought that such people could be employed in the surveillance of ordinary individuals and an even more disturbing one that they were apparently acceptable to, and used by, government agencies.

Meanwhile Tam Dalyell had received the 'considered response' from Giles Shaw who, it will be remembered, had promised to go thoroughly into the whole business however long it took. In the event it took him just nine days. The response was in the form of a letter which states, 'I am now able to state unreservedly that your allegations about the security services being involved are totally without foundation.' This statement was actually made *before* the police undertook any inquiries to discover whether or not any of Dalyell's allegations might possibly be correct.

Tam's reaction was, 'This is just typical of the whole *Belgrano* saga: claims are dismissed before they have been properly considered and then, sooner or later, lo and behold! the claims turn out to be true. I think that Giles Shaw has simply gone through his officials to the security services and asked them and they've said, "There's nothing in it, old boy!"'[3]

Pressed further, on 17 January Shaw produced a more lengthy written reply covering some of the individual points Dalyell had raised.[4] He confirmed that there had indeed been evidence of 'a thorough and systematic search' and also that there had been signs of a struggle. He understood from the Chief Constable

Robert Cozens that the term 'ransacked' was an exaggeration of the true extent of the disorder and 'had not been used by the police in describing the break-in'. The telephone wires had now been 'pulled out', although the police had said originally that the wires had been expertly disconnected. 'Subsequent checks' had caused them to change their minds. The difficulty with this theory is that the screws would have been loosened if the wires had been pulled out of the junction box by force, but according to the telephone engineer this was simply not the case.

Tam was now being leaned upon to drop his research into the Murrell affair. He underwent a three-and-a-half-hour interrogation by Assistant Chief Constable Bernard Drew and Chief Superintendent David Cole, during which he stuck to his story: his source, which he would not reveal, was impeccable and that source had told him that the intelligence services were under intense pressure to find the source of the *Belgrano* leaks and that the operation to track down the culprit had been the result of an inquiry set up by Cabinet Secretary Sir Robert Armstrong. The response from the police was that his intervention was hampering them in the furtherance of their inquiries.

In a letter to Cozens after his interrogation, Dalyell wrote, 'The police should not be content with bland assurances that Intelligence was not involved but should cross-question Sir Robert Armstrong, Mr Peter Marychurch [head of GCHQ, Cheltenham], and some of their subordinates.' In essence Tam Dalyell wanted no stone left unturned. He insisted, again, that he had not been 'set up' by his sources, nor was he lying. 'I have no great faith in lie detectors, but I am quite willing to submit to a polygraph test if you think it will be useful.'

In his reply[5] Cozens said first that he was sure it would be understood that his comments must be limited to the police investigation leaving 'you to pursue the political issues elsewhere. I appreciate that you feel the two aspects are connected, but the nub of this matter is the discovery of evidence to support your view.' A careful assessment of all the evidence Dalyell had provided at his interviews 'has not produced any evidence lending substance to your claim that British Intelligence was linked to Miss Murrell's death . . . The written material you gave my officers consists mainly of a collection of speculative articles, letters or remarks from various sources, but none of it provides any evidence to support what can best be described as rumours.'

In conclusion, while respecting Dalyell's right to protect his source, he said, 'The investigation of a death occurring in these circumstances is an extremely serious matter. If you think your informant has evidence that would assist us, then you have a public duty to encourage the person to come forward. I give you my assurance that any evidence that is forthcoming will be very thoroughly investigated.'

Shortly afterwards Robert Cozens left the West Mercia police force to become a special adviser to Home Secretary Leon Brittan at the Home Office.

January ended with a spectacularly dramatic further coincidence. On Monday 28 January West Mercia Police revealed that two days earlier, on the Saturday before the *Observer*'s story about the agencies involved in the Sizewell surveillance, and the morning after an investigative documentary on local television, there had been a serious fire at Hilda's bungalow at Llanymynech. The Shack had been seen on fire at 8.30 a.m. and the fire brigade called immediately. A police investigation was launched, the building sealed off, forensic scientists called in from the Home Office laboratories in Chepstow and evidence removed for analysis. A police spokesman told the media that the case was being treated as arson.[6]

The following day a spokesman appealed through the local media[7] for assistance from any source and in an apparent contradiction of the previous statement said every option was open, 'including the possibility that it was an accidental fire, perhaps started by a vagrant'.

Another obvious possibility was Welsh fire-raisers, as there had been a spate of arson attacks on English second homes in Wales; early in the proceedings the police did not think this was the case, although subsequently they decided it was possible. However, no nationalist organisation came forward to claim responsibility, as was usual in such circumstances. Neither the motive for the fire nor the culprit has ever been discovered. All in all, January had been a busy month.

Meanwhile visits by unusual burglars, who were not interested in stealing valuables, continued. By this time I had almost finished a short account, to be published in paperback, of what was then known about the Murrell murder and what I considered to be discrepancies between the official version of the police investigation and what appeared to have taken place. On 19 February I was telephoned by another freelance journalist, Grahame Smith, who had decided to write a book on the same subject. After a brief discussion as to the point I had reached and the possible publication date (later put back for totally non-sinister production reasons), Smith rang his own prospective publisher, Cecil Woolf. Woolf runs a small, radical publishing house and had already published two books by Tam Dalyell, one of which had covered the Falklands conflict.

Woolf works from home; Smith had called him at about 8.30 p.m. and they had agreed on a commission. At 11.15 p.m. Woolf and his wife went to bed. In the morning they discovered that their bathroom window had been forced and that the security lock had not only been broken but had disappeared. Nothing had been stolen and it was not possible to tell if any papers had been disturbed. It had snowed during the night, but there were no footprints outside the window as the thief had thoughtfully swept the snow smooth. The Woolfs, who had never been burgled during their previous five years in the house, reported the matter to the police who were unable to throw any light on it.[8]

In March 1985 the two television documentaries already referred to were transmitted, *World in Action* on 4 March and the second *Crimewatch* on the Murrell murder ten days later. There were marked differences in the facilities offered by the police to the two teams of programme makers, apart from the information regarding the telephone mentioned earlier. Stuart Prebble of Granada had asked for permission to film his reconstruction using Hilda's own car but West Mercia Police had refused, saying that it had been dismantled for forensic examination and was still in pieces. It appeared, however, in one piece on *Crimewatch*. Prebble was also asked not to reveal that 'the intruder' had helped himself to a can of Harp lager, that the passenger side of the fascia panel of Hilda's car had been damaged by what appeared to be cuts from a knife and that a grapefruit found in the car had been punctured by the same weapon, as publicising these facts would hinder enquiries;[9] yet in *Crimewatch* the police themselves gave out the information.

World in Action offered a reconstruction with an actress dressed as Hilda. She was shown being frogmarched across a field towards the copse in broad daylight and obviously in full view of some farm cottages. The *Crimewatch* reconstruction suggested that Hilda might have attempted to run away from her abductor after the car slithered to a halt in the lane, which was why her body was found in the copse. *World in Action*'s conclusion was that while there was no definite proof that the murderer was not an opportunist burglar, there was at least a possibility that some kind of a conspiracy had occurred. *Crimewatch* did not even mention such a possibility, preferring to give the official police version of what had happened. In fact they had moved the story on only marginally from their earlier programme the previous July.

During March West Mercia Police, fed up with implied or even overt criticism of the way they had handled the investigation, announced that they would be setting up an internal inquiry under the direction of the Assistant Chief Constable of Northumbria, Peter Smith, and a colleague, Superintendent Cecil Hall.

On the 20th of the month Smith and Hall called on me in my house in Cornwall late in the evening. I was tired, having travelled down from Manchester that day, but agreed to assist them so far as I was able. It was not a fruitful encounter. I willingly explained to them what was in my book but would not give the names of contacts such as the Telecom engineer and the sexual counsellor, as I had promised not to involve them any further. I could also not reveal Tam Dalyell's source as I did not know who it was myself. I suggested they turned their attention to the dubious investigative agencies in East Anglia, but this was not met with any enthusiasm and I was told that the Sizewell side of the business had already been dismissed as a motive. The exchange ended in some acrimony with Superintendent Hall suggesting I saw myself as 'some kind of Cornish Miss Marples', seeking personal publicity, and they left warning me that I was inevitably going to end up making a fool of myself as, by the time the book came out, they would almost certainly have caught the killer. I replied that this was a risk I was prepared to take and that it seemed to me that the last suspects they were prepared to consider seriously were employees of one or other of the investigative agencies. (As a footnote, I am not a betting person but the next day I placed a one-pound bet at 100 to 1 on Last Suspect for the Grand National. It won.)

The Murrell affair rumbled on in the Commons for several months, with the government sticking to its statement that 'there is no evidence to suggest the involvement of British Intelligence officers in the murder', which is almost undoubtedly true, while Tam Dalyell, Paddy Ashdown, Clive Soley and Gerald Kaufman, among others, continued to ask questions.

For a period in the New Year of 1985 and into the spring my post arrived obviously having been tampered with, envelopes having been slit along the bottom and clumsily resealed. Heavy-handed inquiries were made in the Stratford area as to what I was investigating when in fact I was busy researching a book on Jacobean dramatists for the opening of the Royal Shakespeare Company's Swan Theatre, and I received a number of deeply unpleasant telephone calls from two men, one of whom suggested that I dropped any more involvement in the affair, for 'look what happened to Hilda Murrell'. The harassment only stopped after the matter was raised in the House of Commons when Paddy Ashdown had set down an Early Day Motion on the subject, but by the June the overt surveillance, at least, had ceased.

The *Star*, of course, was unable to interview Barry Peachman, who might well have been able to throw some light on the whole Sizewell operation and whose death has remained a matter of speculation ever since.

An ex-MI6 source told the reporters Neil Wallis and Peter Hooley that MI5 had always had a reputation for dirty tricks (not a surprising viewpoint given the long-standing antagonism between the two organisations), but what is undoubtedly true is his statement, made before the Peter Wright affair, that 'some Intelligence officers don't even bother to apply for clearance, they just do it. And now, coupled with the worrying lack of proper clearance, they are using what we call the "cut-out" – farming jobs out to private detectives. So the lack of control is almost total – it's a cancer which now affects the whole system. There is no doubt that there has been a considerable downgrading of political control and the effects are too horrific to think about.'

At about the same time the police inquiry, conducted for the West Mercia force by Assistant Chief Constable Peter Smith, concluded its investigation and West Mercia Police duly held a press conference to mark the event. It was made clear from the outset that most of its findings were to remain completely confidential for operational reasons. However, during his ten-week investigation, Smith said he had spoken to various members of the Intelligence Services 'at the highest level'; to Tam Dalyell, who had been unable to come up with a single named source; to Commander Robert Green and to a number of other people. He had also spoken to members of the various investigative agencies mentioned by the media in connection with Sizewell and he had seen the 'list of targets, but Miss Murrell was not on it'.

He had only three criticisms to make of the way West Mercia Police had handled the affair: that they had failed to institute a search for Miss Murrell's body for three days; that they should have followed up speculation regarding the role of Sapphire Investigations in the Sizewell surveillance; and that they should have handled the media speculation in general over the affair more firmly, with a single senior officer answering all inquiries 'to ensure consistency'.

It was also noted that an 'inexperienced officer' had been sent to Hilda Murrell's house, and that, despite finding the lights on and the door ajar, he did not look inside. The new Chief Constable of West Mercia, Tony Mullett, said he accepted the criticisms with regret, but was personally comforted by the knowledge that 'a totally independent officer of great experience has found only these areas to criticise'.

Smith's concluding words to the media were, 'This is probably the most bizarre murder I have come across. I agree that there are a lot of coincidences and it looks like a can of worms. But when held up to the light, there is not a shred of evidence that British Intelligence was involved.'[10]

Interlude II

Chapter 11

No Further Progress

To a large extent the feverish activity of the early part of 1985 petered out after the West Mercia Police had given their minimalist public response to the results of the internal inquiry. Certainly those investigating the matter unofficially felt that every time a lead appeared promising it almost immediately came to a dead end, as if a door had slammed. However, in spite of the police saying they were satisfied that Hilda's anti-nuclear activities had no bearing on her assault, a number of people received telephone or written requests from the police, including a Bedfordshire man who had a call from his bank informing him that there had been a police inquiry over 'the murder in Shrewsbury' and that they were following up a standing order of Hilda's made out to the Nuclear Weapons Freeze Advertising Committee of which the man was secretary. Chief Superintendent Cole also wrote to the Greenham Women Against Cruise, care of their bank, inquiring about a cheque made payable to Dr Lynne Jones.[1]

The Crucible Theatre in Sheffield put on a play about Hilda in its Studio season, there was a scattering of magazine articles, both in this country and abroad, after which the affair slipped out of the news, overtaken by other events.

★   ★   ★

During the 1980s concern continued to grow over the lack of accountability of the security services and their relationships with private security firms and other freelance bodies devoted to 'countering subversion'. That Margaret Thatcher approved of some of the wilder offshoots of the latter is spelled out in Brian Crozier's *Free Agent*, in which he details his own career and the founding of 'Shield' and the Institute for the Study of Conflict (ISC). Crozier, a right-wing maverick and a fan of both General Franco and Chile's Pinochet, has been a freelance for both MI5 and MI6 and, according to Richard Norton-Taylor, worked for the Foreign Office's shady Information Research Department, an organisation disbanded by David Owen in 1977. Its job was to provide unattributable reports of supposed subversion.[2]

Crozier saw reds everywhere including, like Wright and his band, in the Labour Party: he writes that he had long nursed the notion that the Labour Party was 'irremediably tainted'. Mrs Thatcher was personally involved in the setting up of Shield, an organisation specifically designed 'to counter subversion by clandestine means, both offensive and defensive', Crozier defining subversion as the political equivalent of AIDS. Back in 1978 when she was still Leader of the Opposition, Thatcher chaired a meeting held in an unnamed City bank, attended by Sir Keith Joseph, Lord Whitelaw, Lord Carrington, a member of Hambro's Bank, Edward Leigh (now an MP and recently sacked by John Major as a junior DTI officer) and Crozier himself, during which she suggested that Shield should be officially attached either to 10 Downing Street or to the Cabinet Office. It seems this bizarre notion was vetoed by Carrington.[3]

On at least four occasions while Thatcher was Prime Minister, Crozier was invited to Chequers and had long tête-à-têtes with her during which a wide variety of subjects was discussed. To its credit, MI5 had distanced itself from the operations of Shield and the ISC and had made it clear in no uncertain terms that it preferred to do without Crozier's assistance. It seems, according to his frank revelations, that this attitude, as instanced in the person of the outgoing-head of MI5, Sir John Jones, was openly discussed and criticised at one of these meetings. Crozier felt very sore about his treatment by MI5: 'Indeed,' he writes, 'they [MI5] had carried non-co-operation and non-recognition to the absurd extent of declining even to receive our reports.'

Thatcher, he continues, 'was listening intently. I stressed that in my view, it was absolutely essential, indeed indispensable, to restore the availability of MI5 material to selected recipients. This too, she noted . . .' On other occasions they discussed the miners' strike and the subversive nature of Labour local authorities.[4]

It is easy to dismiss Crozier as just another right-wing meddler: somewhat disarmingly, he quotes the response of MP Brian Magee to an invitation to a special conference he was organising; Magee responded that he considered the views being expressed were 'bonkers'. Yet this man had access to, and the sympathetic ear of, the Prime Minister of the day. Did she share his view that during the 1970s and early 1980s MI5 had abdicated its responsibilities by not pursuing 'subversives' rigorously enough?

Meanwhile further information was coming to light on the activities of the Zeus Securities Group, not least that it appears unpleasant things can happen to those working for it on a free-lance basis after they have left the company. One such person, electronics expert David Coughlan, a specialist in the use of surveillance equipment, admitted on a Yorkshire Television *First Tuesday* programme in 1988 that he had supplied such equipment to Zeus for the Sizewell surveillance back in 1983, including miniaturised tape recorders. He claimed that the operation had been a lengthy one involving a wide variety of people. His particular role had been to fit out undercover agents with secret tape recorders to enable them to spy on the individual Sizewell protesters. Asked who he thought had employed Zeus to carry out the surveillance, Coughlan replied that so far as he knew it was British Intelligence and MI5. He said that he and his colleagues had been told that the aim of the operation was to detect 'sinister subversives' infiltrating the various anti-nuclear groups.

Coughlan had extensive background experience, starting in Army Intelligence and, after he had left the service, in undercover work for the security services. According to a report in the *Observer* he was so well trusted by them that he was asked to supply monitoring equipment for the Thatchers' old flat in Flood Street. In 1987 Coughlan went to prison having been found guilty of tapping the phone of Gerard Hoareau, the Seychelles Opposition leader assassinated in 1985.

Another ex-Zeus freelance who came to grief was Hassan Assali, also an electronics expert, who had worked for a variety of security agencies and had his own specialist firm, Radiofort Sentek Ltd, at Boreham wood. On 30 May 1984 armed police officers and HM Customs agents raided the offices of a North London private security firm, searched the premises and took away what were said to be bomb-timers and unlicensed firearms. Further searches at Radiofort Sentek resulted in the removal of other items and documents.

Finally, Assali was charged with offences relating to the manufacture of timing devices and appeared at St Albans Crown Court in May 1985. Gary Murray says he made contact after recognising the name of the defendant as one associated with a number of private agencies, including the Zeus Securities group. Assali's defence was, and is, that the timers were definitely not designed for use with explosives. He is convinced he was stitched up. Closely questioned both by Murray and later by journalists, he has stuck to his story: that he had worked for Peter Hamilton on and off since 1978, that he has on a number of occasions supplied surveillance equipment to Zeus through an employee, ex-MI5 officer Jeremy Wetherall; that throughout his long association with Zeus in general, and Hamilton and Wetherall in particular, he had believed they were associated with British Intelligence, indeed that both had boasted of their strong links with the security services. He alleges that Hamilton once told him he was confident from his own knowledge of having worked for MI6 that nothing he asked Assali to do could be said to be breaking the law.[5]

Assali is particularly sore that the damaging prosecution technical evidence which helped secure his conviction was supported in court, to his astonishment, by no less a person than Jeremy Wetherall. Indeed, he considers Wetherall's evidence was crucial and is unable to understand why he should have acted as he did. It must be said, though, that it was not only Wetherall's evidence that damaged Assali, but also that of an ex-employee of Assali's who had claimed that he had been asked by the defendant to work on bomb-timers for export orders. The truth of the matter is, as so often in this murky world, unlikely ever to be known.

Certainly Assali at one time did have a close working relationship with Zeus Securities, for he showed Murray a book written by Hamilton with the title *Espionage, Terrorism and Subversion in an Industrial Society,* in which Hamilton had written a personal message: 'Hassan Assali with the author's compliments and thanks for your friendship. Peter Hamilton 24th May 1983.' This was just six days before the first police raid.

In January 1989 Zeus Securities surfaced again. This time the reason was the proposed appointment of Lord Chalfont as Deputy Chairman of the Independent Broadcasting Authority, the IBA. Concern had been expressed in a number of quarters over his suitability for such a position, citing, among other things, his various intelligence connections, his links with the Media Monitoring Unit, founded to expose left-wing bias in the BBC, and his setting up of what had seemed, at the time, to be the mysterious Committee for a Free Britain which published £210,000-worth of hysterical anti-Labour advertising during the 1987 General Election campaign.

On the 25th of the month Liberal Democrat leader Paddy Ashdown wrote to Margaret Thatcher expressing his disquiet at such an appointment, noting that when he had raised the subject in the House the previous week, she had 'expressed surprise that I should even ask'. This was an understatement. His request had reduced her to roaring rage.

In his lengthy letter, Ashdown first refers to the general disquiet over Chalfont being given such a post, after which he turns his attention to the link with Zeus Securities. 'It is a matter of public record that Zeus were engaged by an unknown client for the investigation and surveillance of the objectors at the inquiry into the Sizewell B proposal. Zeus contracted the work to Sapphire Investigations Bureau Ltd.' He then quotes from Zeus's Articles of Association which include the provision of 'advisory and consultancy services to government', after which he points out that Zeus, or one of its companies, contracted out work 'to agents who had criminal records'. He goes on to claim that he has other information regarding Zeus and government departments which he could disclose to her if she wished it.

Chalfont, he continues, joined other directors of Zeus as a director of Securipol Ltd, who shared a registered office and directors with Ensec Ltd, whose 'purpose is the undersea dumping of nuclear waste. Some prominent Conservatives are Directors of Ensec. The objectives of Securipol, as stated in the Articles of Association, are almost identical to those of Zeus.' According to his own information from Companies House, Chalfont was still, at that time, a director of Securipol.

Ashdown concludes by asking the Prime Minister if she was aware of Chalfont's involvement with Zeus and Securipol when he was appointed to the IBA and if not if she would reconsider the reappointment. He also enquires if she thinks it appropriate that someone with such a background be charged with the task of mediating between the interests of broadcasters and the government of the day.

It is not surprising that he never received a satisfactory reply.

In February 1990 newspapers eagerly ran stories to the effect that a man would appear in court in connection with the Murrell murder. The man was David Mackenzie, an unemployed hotel worker with a mental age of nine who had confessed, altogether, to ten murders including those of schoolgirls Susan Maxwell and Caroline Hogg.

The barrister assigned to his case only received the Murrell papers at the last minute and, remembering that there had been a good deal of controversy regarding the case, said that if this charge was to be proceeded with, he would require far more notice. On inquiring how Mackenzie had come to confess to the murder he was told that he had picked out Hilda Murrell from photographs. How many had he been shown, the barrister wanted to know. It transpired he had seen only one and that when asked by the police, 'Did you kill this woman?', he had replied, 'Yes.' Mackenzie was convicted of murdering two elderly women, Henrietta Osbourne, aged eighty-six and Barbara Pinder, aged seventy-six.[6]

His defence lawyers were far from satisfied with the verdict and the case went to appeal where, in July 1992, it was agreed that Mackenzie was what is known as 'a confessor', someone who confesses to high-profile murders: during the time he was remanded in custody it became a standing joke with other prisoners to put him up to confessing to a variety of killings. In spite of this the original verdicts of guilty of the murder of the two named women were upheld. At the time of the appeal the Murrell murder charge still hung over Mackenzie despite the fact that the police, while professing to believe that only one burglar had been involved in the break-in, had for years held evidence showing that the traces of semen found in Hilda's bedroom proved that the man in question had had a vasectomy. Mackenzie had not.[7]

PART IV

The Killing II

Chapter 12

Ceres

It was through her mother, an old friend of Hilda Murrell's, that Catriona Guthrie first made her acquaintance. When she had gone to work in Shrewsbury her mother had urged her to look Hilda up, but for some time she did not do so, feeling somewhat daunted at the prospect of introducing herself to an elderly lady she knew little about, except that she had been an expert rose-grower. However, after being asked to deliver some conservation leaflets to her, she agreed and the two women finally met. They soon became firm friends, drawn together in part by their enthusiasm for a variety of causes from Amnesty International to a wide range of conservation projects. Hilda was, says Catriona Guthrie, amusing, highly intelligent and abrasive, and she did not suffer fools gladly.[1]

Her murder obviously shocked Ms Guthrie, who soon became aware of the rumour and speculation surrounding the affair. She did not volunteer to give information to the police at the time – in part, she says, because she felt she had little useful to say as she had not seen Hilda for a few weeks. Hilda had not mentioned anything to her about feeling threatened, although after the murder she heard that Hilda had expressed such fears to a number of other people. She thought that if the police needed her help they would look her up: they never did.

Over the following years she discussed the case at length[2] with Hilda's friends, with Robert Green and his wife and, through Green, with Gary Murray. But gradually Hilda's death, awful as it was, receded, life went on and she left Shrewsbury, eventually taking up a nature conservancy post in Lincoln. She continued her involvement with Amnesty, however, and she also had a long-standing interest in the plight of the Nagas, the tribe living in the Himalayas close to the Indian border who have an on-going dispute with the Indian government over their right to self-determination. Catriona's mother, in fact, had spent seven years living among them and recording their way of life. Because of this interest it was suggested to her by Amnesty that she might like to contact an inmate in a nearby prison who had spent his time inside studying the Nagas and their political problems. She wrote to the prisoner and was then granted voluntary visitor status so that she could discuss the Nagas with him.

Later, after the prisoner had been released and they were discussing their own background in conservation issues, the name of Hilda Murrell cropped up. Mrs Guthrie was astounded when her contact told her of someone in the prison he had just left who claimed to know a great deal about the Murrell murder. In November 1991 she duly received permission to visit the man in question and discovered that he had shared a cell in York Prison with a man serving fifteen years for armed robbery who claimed to have been part of a team which had broken into Hilda Murrell's house, an operation that had gone badly wrong.

After taking advice from Gary Murray, Ms Guthrie questioned the informant at length over a number of visits, at the end of which, on 10 June 1992, she put all her knowledge into a sworn, sixteen-page affidavit, an edited version of which appears in Murray's book, *Enemies of the State*.[3] The names of those alleged to have been involved in the affair are not revealed in the book.

The prisoner's account consists of what, after corroboration in part from other sources,[4] might be called the core story, plus other information which is more difficult both to believe and to check out.

The core story is this. As we know from other accounts, early in 1984 there was increasing anxiety in Downing Street over the *Belgrano* leaks, culminating on 19 March in what can only be described as panic. Every possibility had to be tried, however remote. At about that time, or even a little before, the connection between the elderly Sizewell protester, Hilda Murrell, and her nephew, Commander Robert Green, had been noted and the simplistic assumption made that he might possibly have passed raw signals data on to her.

It was decided to search her house. A high-powered operation did not appear to be required and it seems that MI5 was bypassed and the work put out to a major agency often used for official business. It was not expected that there would be any real problems. It was known, presumably through phone taps, that Hilda would be out all day on 21 March, which should have given ample time for a thorough search of her house.

The agency in question delegated the job to its northern offshoot, which operated under the name Ceres. The liaison officer between the main agency and Ceres was an ex-MI5 operative also given the name of a Greek deity: Demeter.

Ceres, and through them the main security firm, certainly employed a number of doubtful operatives, including one man who had allegedly been involved in a series of violent crimes going back over twelve years.[5] His legitimate business was that of a garage-owner and he was later described in his local media as 'an inveterate womaniser whose life of crime helped to fund expensive holidays and lavish evenings dining and dancing, while his generosity to his friends and neighbours was legendary', which sounds like pulp fiction.[6] It is now suggested that his amazing run of luck in not getting caught over the years had not a little to do with the assistance he gave to well-placed security firms and his involvement with Ceres.

He was useful to them as an expert breaker-and-enterer who could handle a range of weapons. He had suffered from learning difficulties as a child to the point where he had had to attend a special unit, but he was intelligent and resourceful. He was not the only Ceres employee with criminal connections: there were four others, three men and a woman, all of whom worked regularly for the agency concerned when it wanted something doing of a doubtful nature which could then, if necessary, be disowned afterwards.

Ceres used members of the same group or cell during the miners' strike when they acted as *agents provocateurs* and were involved in a number of notorious, violent incidents.[7]

The assignment on this occasion seemed simple enough – to search Hilda Murrell's house for papers or information relating to signals intelligence, especially anything which might contain specific reference to the Falklands War in general and the *Belgrano* in particular. The most frightening aspect of the informant's story, Catriona Guthrie writes in her affidavit, was that the leader of the group was said to be reporting to the Cabinet Office via a liaison officer with MI5 connections. This was the man known as Demeter.

The team sent down to Shrewsbury were the garage-owner, a woman nicknamed Helga, two experienced members of the team, both with previous form, and a low-life villain with connections with the extreme Right who liked to take the name Spengler. Subsequent investigation points to there possibly also having been an electronics expert involved, but this is not certain. So far as is known, only four of the five actually entered Hilda's house, and only two of them, the garage-owner and the woman, knew exactly what they were looking for. The fifth person, allegedly in overall charge of the operation, was in the area but did not take part in the break-in.

Having waited to make sure that Hilda had left home, apparently for the day, the four let themselves in and either they or somebody else disconnected the green wire from her telephone. They then set about searching the house. At an early stage, the garage-owner discovered the deeds to the Shack and decided that Hilda might well have thought it would be safer to take there any documents she might wish to conceal. He therefore took the decision, as it was not too far away, that he and Helga would conduct a brief search at Llanymynech, leaving the other two to continue going through Ravenscroft on the assumption that, as Hilda was not expected back until at least the end of the afternoon, he had plenty of time to return and carry on the search in Shrewsbury. He then left for Llanymynech, taking Helga with him.

The other two continued with their work and so were taken totally by surprise when Hilda suddenly arrived home. Whether she immediately discovered the intruders or whether some short while elapsed before she did so, we do not know. In any event the two men used a sheet in an effort to wrap her up and a struggle ensued on the stairs during which one of the banister rails was broken. Having been effectively silenced, Hilda was then tied up and dumped on her bed.

Spengler then tried to make Hilda tell him if she had any stolen 'papers'. According to Catriona Guthrie's informant, the other man refused to have anything to do with what followed, which included Spengler punching a grapefruit with a knife to show Hilda what he would do to her, inflicting some minor stab wounds on her arms and half-suffocating her with a wet towel. (Wet towels were found in the house after her abduction.)

Shortly before lunchtime the other two returned, having failed to find papers of any kind at the Shack, and were appalled to discover what had happened, not least the fact that the violence had produced a state of sexual arousal in Spengler who had first tried to force Hilda into having oral sex then, having failed, had masturbated over the bed where she was lying.

The story then becomes considerably less clear and more difficult to believe, although it must be emphasised that Catriona Guthrie is a well-balanced, pragmatic woman, not likely to give rein to wild fantasies, and that she was prepared to swear to what she was told. She does, however, recognise only too well that she might have been made use of or that the account might have been embroidered and acquired extraneous material in the telling. Here the account moves on from the core story.

According to her informant it was not Hilda who was driven away in her car but Helga, wearing Hilda's coat and hat, while Hilda herself, dead or alive, was taken to a deserted airfield used by the USAF during the war and known locally as 'Little America'; she was dumped on the following evening, Thursday, in the copse where she was found. By which time the official intelligence organisations had been contacted to help clear up the whole mess.[8]

One question, among many, raised by this latter information is – even if for some reason it was felt necessary for Helga to impersonate Hilda in the car, why should the car then have been driven past the police station and in such an erratic manner that half Shrewsbury seems to have noticed it. At any time it could have been noticed by police either on foot or in a police car and stopped.

Other problems arise over where the car was found. If Hilda was not in it when it was driven to Hunkington, why bother to bring her there and leave her in the nearby copse? Surely it would have been far more sensible to leave her body near wherever she was taken so that when the car was finally identified and a search instituted, it would have been some considerable time before she was found; indeed it might well have been months. Certainly there is a case for her having been placed somewhere near to the car before being moved later and there is the evidence of the tractor driver and others who saw lights in the copse on the Thursday night and a large and unfamiliar black car parked in the lane.

Catriona Guthrie ends her affidavit: 'I have applied considerable thought to the testimony and credibility of my informant and do of course understand the value of hearsay evidence.

'However, given all the unusual and controversial circumstances surrounding the death of Hilda Murrell, I verily believe that it is in the public interest to activate either a public or judicial investigation into her death, and that in view of the past, unrelated, events involving the use by Security Services of criminals on freelance assignments, serious consideration should be tendered to my informant's statement.

'I would like to conclude by saying that I am fully aware of the offence of perjury and that I swear this affidavit in the sincere belief that the claims of my informant may well be relevant to the murder of Hilda Murrell. I am of sound mind and body and am not making this statement for any pecuniary advantage. The identities of the team said to have been responsible for Hilda's murder, along with the personal details of my informant have been supplied to Gary Murray.

'Finally, I respectfully point out that as a prisoner isolated from society, my informant has no protection and should it ever become known that he has supplied me with this information and assistance, it is more than likely his life will be in danger.'

In *Enemies of the State*, Murray proceeds to give very brief descriptions of the members of the team allegedly involved, and what subsequently happened to them. Team Member 1 is currently serving fifteen years for armed robbery and 'is said to have done a deal in exchange for his silence'. Team Member 2 is serving sixteen years, also for armed robbery, but has now been committed to a special hospital where he is receiving treatment for severe depression. Team Member 3, a 'violent criminal', is 'now deceased after being accidentally shot by his own gun during a police chase'. Team member 4, Helga, has disappeared after serving a two-year prison term, and Spengler has also vanished.

Following the book's publication, the West Mercia Police announced they would be re-opening the investigation into the Murrell murder in the light of the information in it. For some time Guthrie and Murray withheld the names of those allegedly involved in the Ceres operation in the hope that some kind of judicial inquiry might be undertaken but when it became clear that this was extremely unlikely, Murray, after discussion with Triona and having taken legal advice, wrote to DCI Peter Herbert, by recorded delivery, on 25 September 1993, naming not only all those allegedly involved in the break-in, but the Ceres liaison officer and Triona's initial informant as well. The information was not acknowledged until 1 November. However, by the early autumn, other people were also trying to discover for themselves the identities of those supposedly involved.

Chapter 13

Aftermath

As there have not been many cases of death following police chases in the relevant part of the country, it was not too difficult to go through what there were and discover the identity of Team Member 3. Interestingly, the artist's impression of this man, published when he was being hunted for killing a policeman, is almost identical to the first artist's impression of the running man in the Murrell case. His name was David Gricewith.

On 31 October 1984, six months after Hilda's death, David Gricewith and another man set out to rob a Leeds Post Office. Whether the police were there by chance or had been tipped off is not recorded, but in any event the two policemen concerned tried to arrest the men as they were in the act of stealing a vehicle parked outside a local church. While resisting arrest, Gricewith pulled out a .38 calibre revolver and shot first at Police Constable John Thorpe, wounding him in the stomach, then at Sergeant John Speed, killing him. Both men then ran off.

Immediately an enormous police hunt for the killer was organised and, very early in the proceedings, Gricewith was interviewed but convinced police, backed up by an alibi from his girlfriend, that he had not been in the area at the time. Two people (neither of whom is Murray), unknown to each other and quite independently, have alleged that following his questioning by the police, Gricewith felt the need to get out of his home area for a short while and disappear. He then remembered Hilda's Shack at Llanymynech, drove down to North Wales and, discovering it still to be unused, spent some time there. One of the two sources has not been concerned with the Murrell murder in any way but came across the information while researching a quite different story. Before Gricewith left the Shack in January 1985 he either burned any traces of his occupation, thus causing the widely reported fire, or tried and failed to set fire to the bungalow and destroy it altogether.[1]

Gricewith was also fortunate in that the police were absolutely convinced they knew who had shot the two policemen and that it was not Gricewith. The man in question, Anthony Kelly, an Irishman who had lived at one time in Leeds, had a history of armed robbery and was by that time serving a fourteen-year sentence for the abortive kidnap of Mrs Jennifer Guinness. Their view had been reinforced by the artist's impression, drawn with the assistance of Constable John Thorpe once he had recovered from emergency surgery. West Yorkshire Police, therefore, struggled to get Kelly extradited from Ireland for questioning not only about Speed's murder but in connection with a number of other armed robberies: they were convinced he had carried out twelve years of successful criminal activity in the area.

They stuck to their view for months, even though it is now clear that several people, including Gricewith's girlfriend, say they knew Gricewith was the killer. The mistaken identification is still shrouded in confusion, for when PC Thorpe recovered from his wounding, so far as he ever did, he was almost certain that it had been Kelly who attacked him. By the summer of 1985 police had prepared a thousand-page dossier on Kelly for the Director of Public Prosecutions with a view to speeding up extradition; one still unexplained fact is that on the day of the policeman's murder a van stolen by an alleged killer was seen parked outside the home of Kelly's former wife in Leeds.[2]

So Gricewith returned to running his garage where neighbours described him as 'a well-established and well-liked member of the village community of Tholthorpe'. Indeed, it seems that Gricewith had managed his double life most successfully. He was said to be 'generous' if 'a bit of a lad', being extremely successful with women; girlfriends were treated lavishly, one being taken on holiday to the Seychelles.[3]

However, according to Murray, the débâcle over the Murrell murder and the alleged shooting of the policemen had been too much for Gricewith's shadowy employers and there is no trace of his having been used on undercover assignments again.[4] Indeed, it is possible to conjecture that they might just have played a part in what happened next.

On 12 February 1987, Gricewith drove his car into the car park of a Presto supermarket in Norton, near Stockton-on-Tees in Cleveland. Here, depending on which account you believe, he was either seen fortuitously by a policeman taking part in a large-scale operation codenamed Vanguard, involving general surveillance of major supermarkets in the Cleveland and Durham areas, or he was the object of a special exercise designed specifically to catch him.[5]

Gricewith had stolen a Ford Escort in which to carry out an armed raid on the supermarket. As soon as he drove the car into the car park he realised he was under surveillance and so immediately turned round and drove away. Teams of police were alerted and he was chased by a police Fiesta. As it caught up with him he stopped the Escort, got out and fled on foot, taking with him a sawn-off shotgun and a Browning automatic pistol.

As the Fiesta came up behind him, he turned and fired at it, stopping the car and shattering the windscreen. He then dragged its driver, a woman police constable, out of the driving seat at gun point, got into the car and drove off in it, hotly pursued by this time by other police vehicles.

He was then chased into a nearby council estate where he was rammed by a police van, causing him to career across a pavement and knock a pedestrian into the air. In his struggle to regain control of the car, Gricewith ploughed into a brick wall. It is then, it is said, that the fatal accident took place as the sawn-off shotgun, which had been lying across his knees, went off, fatally wounding him in the stomach.[6] He was taken into custody and died some time later.

At the subsequent inquest, held in Middlesbrough in September 1988, the police evidence was that after the crash Gricewith had stumbled out of the car and was seized by them and thrown to the ground, where he struggled so violently to break away that it took several officers to pin him to the floor. Detective Constable Kenneth Dunn said he had had to hit Gricewith in the stomach with the butt of the shotgun to quieten him down. He said that he had not realised Gricewith was injured, there was no sign of any blood and Gricewith did not complain that he was in pain.

'I saw him climbing out of the vehicle. He stumbled on to the ground and two police officers jumped on top of him. I saw a shotgun on the ground. I saw that both hammers were closed, giving the impression that it had been fired. He was struggling violently. I struck him in the stomach with the butt of the gun and he quietened down. He was a big man and appeared to be strong. I did not see any injuries whatsoever on Gricewith.'[7]

Detective Constable Sidney Smith, one of the officers who restrained Gricewith on the ground, said that when he got out of the car he was holding his arms across his chest and complained of having broken a rib. He noticed holes in Gricewith's jumper but 'thought this was because it was old. I saw no blood at all.' PC Eric Young, who also grappled with Gricewith after the crash, said that the man had said, 'It's OK, I'm dead', at which he had assumed he meant he was caught and likely to face a long prison sentence. 'I never thought for one minute that he was dying. Now I think he meant he was badly injured.'[8]

Eye-witness Andrew Weatherley, who tried to stop Gricewith

by putting his own van across the road, saw him get out of the crashed car 'clutching his chest. I could see he was pretty injured. He was dragging his feet. Several police officers grabbed hold of him and pulled him on to his back and tried to get his hands off his chest.' Other witnesses said they heard an explosion seconds after Gricewith crashed the Fiesta.[9]

Another police officer, PC Ian Richardson, who had first noticed Gricewith in the Presto car park, said that when he arrived on the scene he saw a hole in Gricewith's jumper with bloodstains showing. However he did not show any sign of serious injury until he was taken to Stockton Police Station and put in a holding room where he sat on a bench. However 'his condition started to deteriorate and it was then we realised he was wounded and an ambulance was called for. I gave him mouth-to-mouth resuscitation until the ambulance arrived.'[10]

A pathologist, Dr Harvey McTaggart, told the inquest that the wound was such that the officers might well not have noticed it, as there was very little blood and Gricewith was wearing a dark red sweatshirt. He said it was not unusual for a person under stress to be severely injured and not realise it. Following a post-mortem examination he had concluded that the gun went off as Gricewith was hurled forwards when the car hit the wall and that even if he had been operated on immediately he would still have died, such were his injuries. In this he was supported by a second pathologist, Dr Alan Usher.[11]

The Cleveland Coroner, Mr Michael Sheffield, commended the police officers for their bravery in tackling a man who had already shown he was prepared to use a gun, and said that they could not be blamed for not realising he was as severely injured as he was. He described Gricewith as a ruthless, violent and highly dangerous criminal, who was also competent and clever. The verdict was Accidental Death caused when his sawn-off shotgun exploded into his stomach at the end of a police chase.

Immediately both the local and national media were flooded

with stories of crimes alleged to have been committed by Gricewith, including thefts of jewellery and cash and ending with a whole series of raids on supermarkets in Stockton, Darlington and Middlesbrough in which tens of thousands of pounds' worth of cash were stolen. In all he is said to have been involved in more than thirty armed robberies and the theft of over £335,000 in cash. The police also revealed that they had found a cache of fifty firearms at Gricewith's home, including a sub-machine gun and 6,000 rounds of ammunition.[12]

Gricewith's death leaves a lot of unanswered questions. Why, if he had so obviously carried out years of armed robberies in the north of England, had he never been caught? He appears to have led a charmed life. Certainly, it is clear that those among whom he had lived for virtually all his life – his grandfather had been the village saddler – had never suspected him of any such thing. His fame, such as it was, was as a first-class garage man: he was known locally as 'the Mechanic'. And if the second version of why the police were staking out the Presto car park – that they were specifically awaiting his arrival – is the right one, then how were they tipped off that he had planned to do a raid that particular day?

In the nineteen months after the shooting of Gricewith and the inquest there were a number of arrests. Five days after Gricewith's death, a man called Paul Guest gave himself up to the police and he and his wife were later interrogated in their home. After his arrest, Guest confessed that he had been with Gricewith when he shot the two policemen. He was charged with the murder of Speed and the attempted murder of Thorpe, to which he pleaded Not Guilty, and with conspiring with Gricewith to rob a Post Office and carrying a firearm with intent to commit robbery; he also pleaded Not Guilty to these lesser charges.

Guest's defence counsel told Leeds Crown Court in January 1989 that his client had been appalled at what had happened but had stood by his friend and lied repeatedly, denying all knowledge of the shootings. He told the police, 'I was there. I could not believe what was happening with people, policemen, getting shot. I was petrified, mortified and was welded to the spot.' That was why he had remained silent for so long. Gricewith had shot first at Thorpe, leaving him wounded in the stomach, then at Speed at point-blank range.

The plan had been to rob a Post Office van, to which end they had needed to steal an unmarked vehicle. It was while they were doing this that they had been intercepted by the police. Thorpe, who had since left the police force, then gave a graphic description of the shooting of Speed and his own wounding. Guest was found not guilty of the murder, but sent to prison on the other charges. His wife Alison, accused of accepting a thousand pounds from Gricewith for withholding information as to his involvement in the shootings, then changed her plea to Guilty, saying that she was horrified to think she had allowed her son to stay in Gricewith's home.[13]

On 17 April 1988, Peter Sanderson, a forty-two-year-old builder from York, appeared in Teesside Crown Court accused of armed robbery. After his arrest, the jury were informed, he had told the police that he had known from soon after it happened that Gricewith had shot Speed and Thorpe and had admitted as much to him. Gricewith had boasted about how he had walked away from the scene of the crime and had later convinced the police that he had had nothing to do with it. He had been visited by two policemen, one of whom, after hearing what he had had to say, had said to the other, 'He doesn't sound like a cop killer to me, does he to you?' Sanderson had gone on to say that Gricewith had scared him. He was accused of a string of armed robberies, some in partnership with Gricewith, and charged with thirteen offences. He pleaded guilty to twelve, was found guilty of all of them and sentenced to fifteen years in prison.[14]

'Woman Jailed for Aiding Killer' ran the headline in the *Daily Telegraph* shortly after the inquest: 'Headmaster's daughter Adrienne Robinson gave armed robber David Gricewith a false alibi after he shot Sergeant Speed in Leeds in 1984. She also acted as getaway driver for Gricewith who carried out more than twenty armed hold-ups between 1974 and 1987.' She was, however, acquitted of a number of other charges. She, too, had been arrested after Gricewith's death.[15]

Information with regard to the other four people allegedly involved in the Ceres operation has been more difficult to ascertain, although their names are now known to a number of people. The man described by Murray as Team Member 1 refused to speak either to him or to anyone else on the subject. However, Murray himself interviewed Team Member 2 in the presence of staff at the special hospital where he is being held. The man in question claimed, not unusually in such circumstances, that the prosecution case against him was untruthfully presented and exaggerated; also that he was persuaded to admit to other offences he and his associates had not committed.

After listening to his woes, Murray produced a ten-by-eight picture of Hilda, along with the artist's impression of the running man suspect superimposed alongside another picture of Hilda wearing her famous hat. According to Murray, as soon as the man saw the pictures, he reacted violently and then refused to look at them. He said, 'I'm not saying anything, I've said too much already, that's why I'm in here.' Murray next mentioned the names of several people said to have been involved, in one way or another, with the Shrewsbury operation and the murder and, in particular, one person associated with a London security firm whose nickname he used. The man admitted knowing the person in question but refused to discuss his relationship with him any further. When Gricewith's name was mentioned and Murray remarked on the fact that he had, apparently, shot himself at the end of a police chase, the man immediately said, 'That's not true, the police shot him to keep him quiet.'[16] Although how he came to that bizarre conclusion was not clear.

Corroboration of what took place during Murray's interview

with this prisoner has come from a colleague after discussions with prison staff who confirmed Murray's account: that the pictures of Hilda had produced a dramatic effect on the prisoner, that he had reacted with increased agitation during the course of the questioning and that he appeared to have knowledge of the subjects under discussion.[17]

Chapter 14

'Not a shred of evidence . . .'

On 25 February, eight months after the publication of Murray's book with its chapter on Hilda Murrell, West Mercia Police gave a press conference to announce the result of the investigation which had followed the publication of the edited version of Triona Guthrie's affidavit.[1] Their conclusions had already been trailed in a report in *The Times* of 7 February 1994 under the heading 'Police Clear MI5 Over Death', in which Michael Evans, *The Times*' Defence Correspondent, revealed that the police had found no evidence whatsoever to support Triona Guthrie's affidavit. He also stated quite incorrectly, with regard to a possible connection with leaked material concerning the sinking of the *Belgrano*, 'Mrs [sic] Murrell's nephew, Commander Robert Green, was a member of the crew of HMS *Conqueror*, the Royal Navy submarine that sank the cruiser.'

Before the press conference, West Mercia Police issued a press release which did indeed totally discount both the information in the Murray book and Triona Guthrie's affidavit, in which the result of eight months' intensive investigation runs to barely a page and a half of A4. Inquiries, it notes, had now been completed into material concerning the murder of

Hilda Murrell and 'it has been possible to fully resolve all the information and none was found to be of any value in the murder investigation.

'We have visited the Headquarters of the Security Services where we spoke to a senior official. The Service co-operated fully with our enquiries and we are entirely satisfied as a result of these and other enquiries that the Security Service was not involved in the murder of Hilda Murrell and had no knowledge of her prior to her death. Similar enquiries were made with the military, including the Ministry of Defence in Whitehall. Again we are able to say that Hilda Murrell was not known to any military department or indeed West Mercia Special Branch, prior to her death.'

The release states that although Murray and Guthrie had refused to identify either the six-person group allegedly concerned in the murder, or the prison informant, 'they were all identified through police enquiries and interviewed, except one now deceased and eliminated from the murder investigation. On interview the informant of Triona Guthrie detailed his information which does not fully accord with the version produced in *Enemies of the State.*'

Then comes the explanation: 'It was established that one of the group, who is serving a long prison sentence, had seen a comprehensive press article on the murder in late 1989. He has stated that in an attempt to focus media attention on his own wrongful conviction he then concocted a scenario based on the article. He later abandoned the tactic but by that time he had passed on the story to a fellow prisoner who was later to come into contact with Triona Guthrie. The persons featured in the scenario were based on co-accused and a friend of the originator.'

The press conference proper began with Assistant Chief Constable Thursfield informing the assembled representatives of the media and other interested parties that he would first make a statement, after which he was prepared to answer questions on the broader issues, while DCI Peter Herbert, who had been closely involved in the Murrell investigation throughout, would take questions of a more specific nature and would also be prepared to see those interested on a one-to-one basis afterwards.

The Hilda Murrell murder was, he said, the West Mercia police force's 'only undetected murder ever', which is why it had remained a live and ongoing inquiry. Over the years every conceivable facility had been offered to the police, especially by the security services and Special Branch, and with particular regard to the latter there has 'never been any record of Hilda Murrell in any Special Branch file'.

Now, having looked through all past evidence and the new information originating from Triona Guthrie, the police could say with certainty that there was 'not a shred of evidence' to back up any of the conspiracy theories put forward over the years. However, they fully realised that while they had always approached the murder with an open mind, 'we will never be able to convince everyone even if we had the head of the security service herself sitting here'. But those who continued, in spite of everything, to speculate on the involvement of the State must ask themselves what their motives were, as because of this speculation, people who might well have been able to provide the police with help and evidence over the years have been prevented from doing so by fears that the murder had come about due to the intervention of an arm of the State.

Five of the unidentified people listed in Triona Guthrie's affidavit as being responsible for the crime had been identified. The sixth was, unfortunately, dead. In pursuit of their inquiries, the police had used professional investigative techniques to get to the truth, techniques which could not be revealed. Very often this consisted of minor, but crucial, pieces of information but 'there are some things professional investigators have to keep up their sleeves'. However, by using these methods the police were now certain, beyond any shadow of doubt, that the five people interviewed were not the perpetrators of the crime. The story had originated from the 'key player' (Team Member 1), following a detailed article in the press and he had taken the action he had to draw attention to what he considered to be his wrongful conviction. The stories of those questioned had also differed from the information in Triona Guthrie's affidavit and that given in Murray's book, in some cases quite substantially.

The ten-year-old investigation, concluded Thursfield, had suffered from ten years of speculation and he requested, 'Please can we now get on with the job without any more speculation.' The conference was then thrown open for questions, most of which concerned the assurances given by the intelligence organisations, the veracity of the team members interviewed and the credibility of the explanation offered by West Mercia Police.

Was he saying, Thursfield was asked, that all the supposedly new material recently published had been nothing more than a put-up job? Nothing the police had learned, he replied, caused him to believe Hilda Murrell's murder was anything other than a non-political, non-sensitive murder carried out by a burglar who panicked. That encapsulated the police theory and was still 'my best guess – though I keep an open mind'.

Why were the police so certain that the intelligence services had been free and open with them? Thursfield said that he was confident this was the case 'so far as I can be', they had been allowed to look at intelligence files which were in order and so 'that is the end of that.' Surely, though, if the security services had something to hide, then the relevant material might well not have been there? The response to this was that the security services were as keen as the police to clear their names and not to be seen as the 'executioners of the State'. 'There were no gaping holes and my judgement is there was nothing there.'

Could he, Thursfield was asked, name the person who gave him this information? Of course not. Was he or she in a senior position? The question was out of order. One journalist pointed out that no such place as the 'Headquarters of the Security Services' in the plural, as described in the press release, existed, so which particular headquarters had they visited? Again the reply was, 'You are out of order on that sort of question.'

Pressed further as to whether or not they had been given unrestricted access to intelligence files at whichever 'head-quarters' (presumably MI5) they had visited, Thursfield finally answered 'no', but they had been given access to the parts of files which would have contained the relevant details had there been any. When this met with some derision, he added that it was 'preposterous' to suggest that vital information might have been destroyed or removed.

On the question of 'military' intelligence records to which the police had also had access, which military were they referring to? Surely Hilda Murrell would have been on the naval lists because of her nephew Robert Green. This prompted a jokey response from Thursfield that it was highly unlikely that the Royal Navy had the time or inclination to note down the aunts of all naval personnel. It was then pointed out to him that Robert Green, himself present at the press conference, had given his aunt's name to the navy as next-of-kin as both his parents were dead and that he had also given it to Naval Intelligence when he was positively vetted. The police could not say if her name had appeared on 'someone else's file'.

John Osborne of HTV, who was one of the earliest jour-nalists to follow up the Murrell story and consistently the best, reacted incredulously. Were they saying she was not on any record even though she had been a 'fierce anti-nuclear campaigner' and had publicly handed out leaflets against the Falklands War while her nephew was actually serving in Naval Intelligence? This elicited the response that it was her right to do this in a democracy without her name being put on any list.

On the question of the provenance of the team alleged to have carried out the Ravenscroft break-in, why had it been stated in the press release that Murray and Guthrie had refused to give the names of those involved to the police when they said they had? Answering this DCI Herbert said that he had asked both of them for assistance in the June of 1993 and both had refused.

The police therefore had to undertake substantial inquiries to discover the names for themselves. Late in November, he added, Murray had, he thought, passed on to him the names of three of the supposed team. (Unless Murray forged his letter of 25 September and the relevant recorded delivery slip, Herbert's statement does not fit the facts.[2])

Surely, Herbert was asked, it was hardly surprising that prisoners already in jail who were then accused of committing a further very serious crime would be extremely unlikely to admit it? No, it was not uncommon, replied Herbert. If, say, a prisoner was already serving a life sentence, then admitting to another serious crime would only make a marginal difference to him. But these prisoners were not serving life, were they, he was asked. Also, surely it was not unlikely that these people, now aware of what they had started, might well substantially change their stories? All but one of the prisoners, said Herbert, were now out of prison and were, therefore, quite free to respond as they wished. (This is being somewhat economical with the truth. While Team Member 1 remains in prison, Team Member 2 is confined to Rampton and likely to remain there.) Herbert added that some of those supposedly involved denied even knowing each other at the time of the murder, let alone ever having had any connection with the security services. How were the police so sure those concerned were telling the truth? Because of the skilled investigative techniques used.

Osborne then asked if the police, in view of the years of speculation, would support the idea of a public inquiry into the affair? No, Thursfield replied. The police had been 'as open with you as any public inquiry would be' and he personally would be against it in terms of cost alone; such an inquiry might well run into 'millions of pounds' of taxpayers' money. But, persisted Osborne, so far from being open, West Mercia Police had always refused to reveal the results of the 1985 internal inquiry carried out by Northumberland Police, apart from a few peripheral matters. Surely now these, at least, could be published? Thursfield replied that as this had been an internal police inquiry, West Mercia Police were under no obligation to publish its findings.

Don't you realise, said Osborne, that the reason there has been so much speculation over the years is that people just do not believe the police theory of the random 'walk-in burglar. Because what you say simply isn't credible?' Thursfield replied that he did not agree with this view but was prepared to defend Osborne's right to express it!

Osborne's response was to run rapidly through the events surrounding the murder by the walk-in burglar: Hilda's abduction and the disposal of the body six miles away, her car left unchecked in a lane nearby for four days, the state of the house, the mystery surrounding the telephone wires, the search through the house which the police themselves had described as 'systematic', the police constable who spent two hours in the house without realising Hilda wasn't in it – these were, Osborne emphasised, 'bizarre events'. 'All I can say,' responded Thursfield, with some exasperation, 'is that you know your business and we know ours.' Things that might seem bizarre to a journalist were not necessarily bizarre to the police.

Another questioner asked if the police were able to give any proof to back up their statement that the years of speculation had prevented witnesses who might have been crucial to the inquiry from coming forward? Herbert replied that they were. Following the publicity given to Murray's book, they had received a call in their incident room from a man who said he'd seen Miss Murrell on the day of the murder. In the event this had not turned out to be the case, but even so, the speculation had prevented his coming forward for nine years.

Gary Murray then asked how Team Member 1 had come up with the name of the disused airfield, Little America, and was told that the informant had been in the Territorial Army years before and had come across the name then, but as this was going into considerable detail, rather than forming part of the broad sweep of the conference, this question could be dealt with later. With reference to Murray, the police were bound to say that his 'book was not a serious book on this murder', omitting to mention that the Murrell murder made up only one section of it. The book, said Thursfield, had worked to a set hypothesis and therefore was written to reach certain conclusions, whereas the police had an open mind.

Finally he was asked about Tam Dalyell's original House of Commons statement that members of British Intelligence had been involved. Had the MP set out deliberately to mislead the House or had he himself been misled? Thursfield said he was not in a position to answer this except to say that he had no reason to believe Mr Dalyell was anything but an honourable man.

The press conference was held on a day full of news, which is possibly why only the briefest down-page reports of it appeared in the media. But however much West Mercia Police might now wish the whole matter would go away, there remains a host of unanswered questions, apart from those which patently did not receive satisfactory answers at the conference.

No one who has undertaken any investigation into the Murrell affair believes that professional members of any of the intelligence services or Special Branch took part in the break-in at Ravenscroft. All those Ministers, MPs, police spokesmen and informed sources have, strictly speaking, been telling the truth. Indeed, there is at least a strong theory that MI5 was actually bypassed during the panic over the *Belgrano* leaks on 19 March 1984. Therefore asking a 'senior official', yet again, if MI5 was directly involved was bound to elicit the same response, so why, except for public relations reasons, ask it? Nor, speaking of public relations, does it seem sensible to describe a visit to a 'Headquarters of the Security Services' which does not exist.

There have been countless examples of those who have undertaken work on behalf of the intelligence services being swiftly ditched if they are caught. A Channel 4 programme on the Scott Inquiry transmitted on 9 March 1994 featured the Grecian family caught up in the Iraq supergun affair who had gone to court without the trial judge demanding the relative public immunity documents be released. John Grecian, like Paul Henderson in the Matrix Churchill affair, had willingly undertaken to provide information regarding Saddam Hussein and had attended a series of joint meetings with members of both organisations and was deeply upset when, after his arrest, neither of the intelligence organisations was prepared to come to his defence.

West Mercia Police reiterated that Hilda's name was not on the files of their own Special Branch and that this in itself supported the claim of the intelligence services that they did not have it either, since much of the information these agencies hold on file comes from the Special Branch units. But it is common knowledge that the information held on hundreds of thousands of people by MI5 alone, much of it wildly inaccurate, is based on information from all sorts of quarters, not just Special Branch.

And at no time was reference made to the private investigative agencies, the role they might have played, who they might have on file, or even their existence.

The dismissal of the story behind Triona Guthrie's affidavit requires more scrutiny, although the police do not doubt that she sincerely believed what she was told.

Without further information it is not possible to prove that the team described as being employed by Ceres actually did carry out the break-in at Ravenscroft and the subsequent assault on Hilda. That having been said, there is legitimate cause for scepticism regarding the explanation provided by West Mercia Police. While no names were released, the responsibility for originating the story appears to be laid at the door of Team Member 1, who is then to have concocted the whole farrago from a newspaper article published late in 1989 as part of his effort to publicise his belief that he had been wrongfully imprisoned. There was only one major newspaper article on the Murrell murder published at that time and it was in the *Independent* on 18 November 1989. The writer, Amanda Mitchison, is as much concerned at the obsessive effect the murder has had on various people as with the details of the affair and leans heavily towards the anti-nuclear theory, quoting Hilda's friend Don Arnott and Robert Green. She mentions a number of oddballs who have become involved over the years, all of whom are well known. Murray is also mentioned in the piece and is described variously as 'the most hag-ridden person involved' and 'a disaffected private eye and now a part-time journalist . . . who believes that he is being persecuted by the inland revenue and that his publishers, Bloomsbury Press, have suspicious links with the security services.' Mitchison also lists plays, television programmes and a feminist novel, all of which have been inspired by the murder. One section deals, briefly, with some of the events surrounding it.

So the prisoner in question is responsible for a remarkable feat. From Mitchison's piece he was able to come up with a scenario which bears only a passing resemblance to the *Independent* feature and which contains details passed on to Triona Guthrie which not only did not appear in that feature but had never been published anywhere at all, including the stealing of small items of pottery belonging to Hilda. It would tax a thriller writer of considerable experience and ingenuity to 'concoct' (the word used in the press release) such a story based only on the *Independent* feature. The one similarity is that Mitchison claims that Robert Green believes Hilda was driven away by the two intruders who had broken in, one of whom sat in the front passenger seat and wore her hat.

Team Member 1 also had to weave into his scenario a number of his previous criminal associates, including Gricewith, and an employee of a private security agency who acted as a liaison officer; after which he passed the whole lot on to another prisoner, who just happened to be visited by someone whose main object was to discuss the tribulations of the Naga tribesmen but who turned out to have direct links with Hilda

Murrell. He then, we are told, decided to abandon the tactic. If this is all true why on earth did he do it? How could he possibly have thought it might help him to 'focus media attention on his own wrongful conviction'? If it was easily shown to be a pack of lies, then he would do himself and his case no good at all and most likely spend more time in prison for wasting police time, while at worst he would put himself in the frame as an accessory to one of the most notorious crimes of the decade and thus find himself facing a further trial, this time for murder.

Nowhere in the *Independent* article is the Shack at Llanymynech mentioned, only 'Hilda's house in Wales', yet Triona's source told her the Shack was searched by Team Member 3 and his girlfriend. Nor does 'Little America' feature; indeed Mitchison quotes Don Arnott and Robert Green as saying that they had found a disused stable in a secluded corner of a field near the copse at Hunkington where they thought Hilda's body may have been concealed.

There is an explanation which makes more sense. Triona Guthrie was distressed by the response of West Mercia Police both in their press release and at the conference, not least because the prisoner discredited for originating the story, Team Member 1, did not do so. The originator was the man known as Team Member 2. The story first surfaced when Team Member 1 arrived on the prison wing which also contained Team Member 2 and Guthrie's original informant, after which Team Member 2 had shown signs of increasing distress and it was during this time that the story first emerged and was passed on to the informant. It was Team Member 2 who could describe, among other things, the china dogs stolen from Hilda's house. Team Member 1, says Guthrie, could not have accurately described what had happened at Ravenscroft since although he had been in the area, he had never entered the house.

I believe that the West Mercia Police accepted in good faith what they were told by the various intelligence agencies

164

regarding their non-involvement. Also that they believe a specific prisoner concocted the entire Ceres story based on the *Independent* feature, a man who, to draw attention to himself, also chose to involve other prisoners – all of whom, not surprisingly, deny their involvement.

But I also believe that West Mercia Police, having decided almost from the outset that Hilda Murrell was killed by a 'walk-in' burglar, have suffered collectively from a set mind which, in spite of protestations of open minds, has prevented any departure from this view.

Nor have some of the wilder shores of fantasy helped: that as Hilda was murdered at the spring equinox she was the victim of a witchcraft/Satanist killing (a theory given serious consideration by some members of the West Mercia police authority)[3]; that Tam Dalyell was deliberately misled as to intelligence by Paddy Ashdown, who had all along been working for MI6; that Hilda had extraordinary secret knowledge concerning nuclear power known only to a handful of world experts.

But at the end of the day, John Osborne's statement at the press conference gets to the heart of the matter: people do not believe the theory of the walk-in burglar because, in view of what happened, it is simply not credible.

Shortly after the West Mercia police conference a somewhat odd book was published. This was *The Detective and the Doctor* by ex-Chief Inspector David Cole and Dr P.R. Acland. Its sub-title is 'A Murder Casebook', and there is a foreword by Sir Thomas Hetherington KCB, CBE, TD, QC, Director of Public Prosecutions from 1977 to 1987, who gives it his blessing.

The word 'odd' is used advisedly, not least because it might well be considered distinctly odd that a Chief Inspector and a forensic pathologist, who are trailed in the introduction as being so very independent of the Home Office and police force, are portrayed as such close chums. It is written in the most curious gung-ho, *Boy's Own* style, and throughout the exploits of Cole and Acland are described in the third person although no other writer is credited with any input. It reads like a third-rate crime novel. The first case the intrepid pair deal with is the Hilda Murrell murder and it is hardly surprising that the conclusion they both draw is that this was a random murder by an opportunist thief. Those who have sought to make more of it are treated with no small contempt.

However, the last of the seven investigations covered is almost of equal interest. This is what became known as the 'M50 Murder'. On 18 June 1988 Maria Wilkes, who was seven months pregnant, went to phone for help after her car broke down on the motorway. As she was making the call she was stabbed in the neck, pushed into a car and driven over two miles down the road, thrown over an embankment and then left to die. The chapter begins with the kind of dialogue frequently used in the book: 'There's blood on the scene and I don't like the look of it. Can I come out and pick you up? I'll be there in half an hour.' Cole duly rushes off to the scene of the crime to find there was a delay in the discovery of the corpse. 'There are bloody fools in any organisation, but David Cole seemed over-blessed by their presence when it came to finding dead bodies.' However, within minutes Acland has arrived at the location and the dynamic duo are ready for their starring role: 'The detective and the doctor were in business again.' If it were not all so serious it would be farcical.

What is fascinating is that in addition to Cole and Acland being involved in both the Murrell and M50 investigations, DCI Anthony Stanley was playing a similar crucial role. As well as running the Murrell incident room, Stanley also made major policy decisions as to the way the investigation was handled, briefed both police and press, and decided what information was released to whom, and when. He also appeared in person on the second BBC *Crimewatch* programme.

In November 1988 Eddie Browning, a nightclub bouncer who had left his home in Wales on 17 June after a row with his wife, was found guilty of the murder of Maria Wilkes.

Evidence against him was thin, not least because whoever abducted and killed Maria Wilkes stabbed her in the jugular vein, causing her to lose some four litres of blood, and yet no trace of blood was ever found in Browning's car.

What proved crucial in the conviction of Browning was the testimony of an off-duty West Mercia policeman, Inspector Peter Clarke, who recalled seeing a silver car pull in behind a pregnant woman who was using a motorway phone. What Shrewsbury Crown Court was never told – nor the Defence – was that in an effort to recall the number of the car, Clarke underwent two hypnosis sessions carried out by Dr Una Maguire. These were recorded on video and the film shows Clarke recalling that he saw a silver-grey saloon, not a hatchback car with chrome bumpers, registration number C858 HFK. Browning's car was a silver Renault hatchback C754 VAD with plastic bumpers. When it came to the trial, Clarke told the Court only that he had seen a silver-grey car with a registration beginning with C and that he could not remember the rest of the number.

Browning's first Appeal, in 1992, was turned down but as more and more information began to filter out and after a sustained campaign by journalist Paul Foot, the case went to Appeal again. Among the witnesses who were not called at the first trial was one who was sure she had seen Maria Wilkes' murderer emerging from the undergrowth and who had told the police, after an identification parade, that it definitely was not Browning. Four others failed to pick out Browning at identification parades. One witness who was called gave a description of a man which could have fitted Browning. By the time he reached Court he had added that he had seen a car with a registration number beginning C7.

Browning had always maintained that he crossed out of Wales over the Severn Bridge, not the M50, but two other separate pieces of evidence which appeared to confirm that this was indeed the case, and that he crossed at approximately

7.36 p.m. (at the time Maria Wilkes was being murdered) were disallowed by the Appeal Court.

On 13 May 1994, Eddie Browning's Appeal was permitted on the grounds, according to Lord Chief Justice Taylor, that there were material irregularities in the way the original investigation and trial had been conducted. Of the witness who told the original Court that he had seen a silver car with a registration number beginning C7, the Lord Chief Justice said: 'The grounds of Appeal contended that the witness had been fed a registration number. That contention . . . was unarguable.' Regarding the video of Clarke, he said they could not be sure the original jury would have reached the same decision had the material irregularities not occurred. DCI Anthony Stanley was particularly picked out for criticism, essentially for attempting to reinforce witness statements and other substantial witness irregularities. The Court was told that a disciplinary tribunal was still pending against Stanley and another, unnamed but retired, police officer.

As Browning was released, Assistant Chief Constable David Thursfield faced the cameras. He expressed no contrition. Indeed, speaking with what Browning's solicitor, Jim Nichol, described as 'cruel arrogance', he said that West Mercia Police were 'disappointed and surprised' at the result of the Appeal and that, after being in Court throughout it, he could see no new lines of inquiry.

Many of those who commented on the result of the Appeal made the point that high profile murder investigations put extreme pressure on police to get a quick result and that it is all too easy for them to focus on what they see as the most likely solution and then move heaven and earth to make it stick.

This theory certainly fits the Murrell murder and all that has happened since, not least the latest investigation into the new evidence. The result of the M50 Appeal, involving so many of the same officers, does not make for confidence in the result of that inquiry, during which, at the press conference described previously, Thursfield referred to Hilda's murder as the force's 'only undetected murder ever'. He can now add that of Maria Wilkes to his list, the case which Cole and Acland had bragged about in their book: 'The detective and the doctor were in business again.'

Chapter 15

Cover-Up

That the random burglar theory lacks credibility in view of the sequence of events surrounding Hilda Murrell's murder is not the only reason why there has been continued speculation over the years and why so many people find the various official explanations so hard to believe. Now there is even more scepticism. The explanation for this is also simple: that in view of all that has surfaced on so many other issues in the intervening years, little credence is placed on any government/official explanations of almost anything you care to name. 1984 marked the high point of the Thatcher administration, the apex of the 'one of us' philosophy and the fight against 'the enemy within'. Large numbers of people went along with it: not any more. Ten years on, public cynicism regarding government probity and, in view of the spate of miscarriages of justice police investigations, has become almost total. The adjective used most often now is 'sleaze'.

The *Belgrano* cover-up was all about preventing it becoming known that Margaret Thatcher had misled both public and Parliament as to the facts of the matter. The priority was to protect the Prime Minister's squeaky-clean image at all costs; so it was that the whole elaborate edifice of deceit was erected and, outside the ranks of the small number of those with a particular interest in the subject, it succeeded. The image survived: that Margaret Thatcher, whatever her faults, always told the truth straight from the shoulder.

Subsequently it was an image which was to become increasingly tarnished as example followed example of the Prime Minister, her government and her advisers being at best 'economical with the truth'. The *Belgrano* cover-up was the start of a slippery slope.

The farcical *Spycatcher* saga came about simply as the result of the disaffection of an ex-MI5 officer, Peter Wright, then living in Tasmania, who was annoyed at what he perceived to be an unfair pension entitlement. The book, though, cannot be said to be amusing. It gives a detailed, and somewhat chilling, account of a career spent entirely in that secret world which surrounded the Murrell affair, reveals details of operations and how they were conducted and repeats an allegation, which had already surfaced many times before, that Roger Hollis, ex-head of MI5, had actually been a Soviet spy. All this would have been bad enough, but what was truly shocking was Wright's unashamed admission that he and a group of MI5 operatives had, during the 1970s, attempted to destabilise and bring down Harold Wilson's Labour government. The embarrassed official response to this was that Wright and his chums had been no more than a few loose cannon, but from later publications it seems that they were not alone in their bizarre belief that during the 1970s half the Labour Cabinet and MPs were, in common parlance, in receipt of sacks of Moscow gold: reds not only under the bed but running the country.

The allegations concerning Hollis had appeared in some detail in 1981 in an earlier book written by Chapman Pincher[1] and had subsequently been denied by Margaret Thatcher in Parliament. She had already vetoed a number of books on security issues and was now determined that Wright's book be stopped. Yet her attitude was, at the very least, inconsistent, since it soon became known that the information on Hollis in

Pincher's book had come from Wright and that a small group of Ministers close to Thatcher had known this all along – as Hugo Young points out in *One of Us*, this meant it had been published with what amounted to government approval.

Every effort and hundreds of thousands of pounds of tax-payers' money, that commodity so carefully nurtured when decisions had to be made about the country's infrastructure, were thrown into a last-ditch attempt to prevent the book's pub-lication in Australia. Cabinet Secretary Sir Robert Armstrong himself was despatched to face a robust interrogation in the Supreme Court of New South Wales by a lawyer singularly unimpressed with the hierarchy of the British Civil Service, during which he made his famous response about being eco-nomical with the truth. The government looked ever more ridiculous as the book began to appear all over the world, while increasing numbers of copies were smuggled into this country from abroad as if they were hard-core pornography.

There followed the unedifying sight of Ministers and officials blaming each other for the mess, with the then Attorney General claiming he had been kept in ignorance of mat-ters directly affecting him. 'And,' as Hugo Young writes, 'presiding over this unseemly spectacle, was a Prime Minister who, having failed to control the original crisis posed by the Pincher book stood firm on her own conviction that however many courts found against her, she had a duty to fight the case until the last drop of taxpayers' money had been expended to defend the principle that spies should not talk. What some called stubbornness, even vanity, she referred to as her bounden duty.'[2]

But during the three years of the *Spycatcher* débâcle, from 1985 to its eventual publication in 1988, cracks were beginning to appear in that façade so carefully constructed around the *Belgrano* sinking. Not least of these was the 'Westland affair'. Ian Gilmour, in his book *Dancing with Dogma*, puts at least some of the unpleasant climate of the times down to what he describes as the 'Thatcher-and-Ingham act', the particular use made by Thatcher's press officer, Bernard Ingham, of the non-attributable Parliamentary lobby briefings which led, on a number of occasions, to Thatcher saying one thing in the House of Commons, while Ingham briefed his favoured journalists with a different version of events outside. Former government minister Sir John Nott described the use of the lobby in this way as 'sickening, deplorable and malicious'. The government news service, writes Gilmour, was subordinated not just to party, but to personal, advantage. 'By the abuse of the lobby system which shields the identity of the briefer, the "news" was being managed and massaged for the benefit of the Prime Minister. Mr Ingham could spread as much poison as she wanted without ever being called to account for his words.'

The Westland crisis, he notes, almost brought about a long-overdue Nemesis to the double act; that it did not do so was directly due to the incompetence of the Opposition.

The trouble arose over the future of the then ailing Westland Helicopter company and a possible rescue in the form of a joint deal with either a European or an American aviation company. Michael Heseltine, then Minister of Defence, wanted a European solution to the problem and had begun to set up a European consortium. Leon Brittan, who had been moved from the Home Office to Trade and Industry in a government reshuffle, preferred the American package. It is clear that the Prime Minister also favoured the latter solution.

On 3 January, Thatcher and her staff had sight of a letter from Heseltine to the consortium which she considered to be provocative. We are then led to believe that her staff conceived the notion of writing to the Solicitor General, Sir Patrick Mayhew, asking him to consider Heseltine's letter; if he agreed there were inaccuracies, he should write to Heseltine pointing them out. Gilmour states that there was only one possible reason for asking Mayhew to write such a letter: so that it might be leaked to the media.[3]

After studying the Heseltine letter, Mayhew duly wrote to the Defence Minister, informing him that one sentence contained 'material inaccuracies' and sent copies of what he had said to 10 Downing Street and to Leon Brittan. Unaware of what was going on, Heseltine read Mayhew's comments, then telephoned him to say he would come back with a considered response.

Those wanting to leak the letter found there was a problem: the convention that advice from law officers is confidential; but the decision was taken regardless and the letter leaked to the Press Association. In the ensuing furore, Mrs Thatcher announced that while she 'regretted' the leak, the information contained in the letter needed to be publicised before a crucial Westland press conference at 4 p.m. that day. The law officers were furious and demanded an inquiry; Sir Robert Armstrong once again found himself in the public spotlight as he undertook the nine-day charade of inquiring into a matter, the truth of which was already known in the Prime Minister's office.

It soon transpired that the letter had actually been leaked by the DTI Press Officer, Colette Bowe. What has never been satisfactorily explained is what happened before she did so. Bernard Ingham said she had told him on the telephone that she had ministerial permission to leak the letter and when he, Ingham, had expressed reservations, Colette Bowe had suggested he leak it himself. He had refused as 'he had to keep the Prime Minister above that sort of thing'. Ingham also maintains he did not inform Thatcher of what was going on which, notes Gilmour, 'in view of their very close relationship is very surprising'.

The version of the Armstrong inquiry is different: the leak had come about due to a misunderstanding between the civil servants involved, a solution, notes Gilmour again, 'that was as convenient as it was implausible'.

The third version, that of the Department of Trade and Industry, is more robust. According to them, Ingham phoned Colette Bowe, told her that he did not want the leak to come from No. 10 and ordered her to give it to Chris Moncrieff of the Press Association. She refused three times, after which, according to one account, Ingham said, 'You will **★★★** do as you're told!' Ingham says this is a lie. Whatever the truth of the matter, Colette Bowe, after further consultation with colleagues and still deeply unhappy, finally informed Moncrieff.

The Westland affair brought about two ministerial resignations, Heseltine's over the way he felt he had been treated, and Brittan, who took on the role of scapegoat. The lady remained firmly in place. The opportunity to expose the dishonesty of what had happened was handed to Neil Kinnock on a plate; in the subsequent parliamentary debate, he blew it and Thatcher was, once again, off the hook. The Westland affair, comments Gilmour, 'marked, as far as we know, the low sleaze mark of the Thatcher administration'. He was writing before the Scott Inquiry hearings.

In a television programme transmitted in 1989[4], Leon Brittan stated categorically that both Ingham and Thatcher's special adviser, Charles Powell, had approved the leak. 'There is no question of the release of that document without the express approval of No. 10.'

Writing on the Westland affair, Hugo Young notes that after it, Thatcher's staff 'and especially Ingham and Powell became almost indissolubly linked with her, almost as if they were a praetorian guard. They became linked, as it were, in a society for mutual protection. People became aware, as they were not during the controversy surrounding the sinking of the *Belgrano*, of the lengths to which Thatcher was prepared to go, not only to be seen never to have been wrong about anything, but also to save her own skin. It also destroyed the image of Thatcher as the politician who told the truth.'

As Hugo Young says of the phrase 'economical with the truth': 'After all, it only described what went on every day in any bureaucracy. It was almost a truism. And yet nobody could deny that, coming from those lips at that particular time, after Westland and in the middle of a host of business done in the secret world, it had a peculiar resonance. The moment it

175

was said, it tied itself to the man who said it – but also to the woman he served. It struck such a jarring chord with the protestation she had so often made that she, unlike almost all others of her kind, always told the truth, the whole truth and nothing but.'

Since then, of course, has come the Matrix Churchill scandal and the hearings before the Scott Inquiry into why arms were knowingly sent to Saddam Hussein, arms later used against our own troops in the Gulf War, and why it appeared that government Ministers were prepared to see men go to prison rather than admit to knowing what had gone on. Thatcher's performance before the inquiry in November 1993 was a remarkable one, during which we were given to believe that the most hands-on Prime Minister in decades did not bother herself with such mundane matters as the relaxation of the rules governing arms sales to a deeply unpleasant Middle Eastern regime against which there was an arms embargo.

The subsequent scandals – *Spycatcher*, Westland, Matrix Churchill, the most recent arms-for-aid business over the Pergau dam in Malaysia, the sleazy lies told by Ministers to save their own skins – all of these are relevant to the Hilda Murrell story. When the thirty-year limitation period ended on the documents connected with the Profumo affair (some of which have still been withheld) it was discussed almost as if it were a quaint notion that Profumo had resigned because he had lied to Parliament. Ministers can lie their heads off these days but it is no longer expected that merely being caught out should lead to any kind of sacrifice.

So many of the leading protagonists in the Wright and Westland affairs appear in the Belgrano saga – Heseltine, Leon Brittan, Sir Robert Armstrong and, of course, Margaret Thatcher herself. Surrounding them have been the banks of advisers, public relations people, civil servants and, last but not least, the non-accountable intelligence services. If those at the top and those who serve them have been economical with the truth on so many subsequent occasions, why should what any of them say be believed in the context of the murder of Hilda Murrell?

Chapter 16

Questions

By mid–1985 those of us who had spent months looking into the events surrounding the Murrell murder on what might be called a professional basis thought it unlikely we would ever know the truth of the matter, not least because each time a lead had appeared promising – such as the revelation of the part played in anti-nuclear surveillance by the private security firms – an invisible barrier seemed to come down preventing that avenue being followed any further. Failing, therefore, the emergence of some brave whistle-blower, that seemed to be that. My own opinion was that if it was some kind of unofficial intelligence operation, carried out by freelances, that went wrong, then Hilda's unknown assailant might well have met the fate of Dennis Lennon, the Special Branch informer, and either been found dead in a ditch at the other end of the country or gone to help make the foundations of the M25.

As Osborne said at the recent press conference, the marginal amount of material released by the West Mercia Police following the 1985 inquiry by the Northumberland force proved to be of little value. Those things most urgently requiring a response had not received one on the grounds that the information was too confidential to be revealed. So many discrepancies were never touched on. Conflicting police accounts were put down either to inexperienced officers or to lack of an overall press-release policy. Specific discrepancies such as whether or not the police walked into, or broke into, Hilda's house were never explained. Nor was the fact that, according to a constable's own account, he had spent two hours at the scene of a serious crime without thinking there was anything odd (only that the first occupant was untidy), and without even being aware, or checking, that the occupant was actually there. This was due, the inquiry had concluded, to the officer's inexperience.

There were no answers at all as to the true state of the telephone wires – had they been expertly cut or yanked out of the wall? A policeman on *Crimewatch* standing in front of a piece of wall holding some telephone wires months after the event could hardly be considered proof either way. Why, after so many appeals for witnesses, were some of those who proffered information apparently ignored?

As for the reassurances of Home Office Ministers and spokespersons for the intelligence services that they were not involved, it hardly takes a Sherlock Holmes or an Inspector Morse to deduce that they would say that whatever the truth might be. They always have and they always will.

Looking at what came out during the twelve months following the murder and relevant information since, it has been possible, as this book has shown, to develop both the nuclear and *Belgrano* threads and their implications. In both cases all the old questions and many new ones remain to be answered.

The Nuclear Connection

Few people, though there remain some, now consider that Hilda's house was searched and she herself murdered as a result of her anti-nuclear views. On this one point it is possible to agree with West Mercia Police. However, all the interesting and relevant information arising out of this having been a possibility, came not from the investigations carried out by the police but from the persistence of journalists. A wide range of views have been expressed with regard to Gary Murray and his book, but it was he who first alerted journalists to the activities of the shadowy and shady agencies employed in carrying out surveillance of nuclear protesters. It is inconceivable that this information would ever have come from the police – they actually had to be informed that it had taken place and prodded to follow it up.

The emergence of these shadowy agencies and their unrestricted activities has raised issues which have a significance well beyond that of the Murrell murder – and more unanswered questions.

Zeus Securities, entrusted with the task of setting up the surveillance in the first place, certainly boasted a splendid array of establishment figures on its board but was quite happily prepared to sub-contract a large part of the work out to Barry Peachman, who appears, from what has emerged and from those who knew him, to have been keen to take it on but was entirely out of his depth. Zeus appears not to have checked that he in turn then passed on much of it to a convicted child-abuser and Nazi sympathiser whose other line was peddling Hitler memorabilia. Meanwhile, as we have seen, two of Zeus's freelances, David Coughlan and Hassan Assali, wound up serving lengthy prison terms. Coughlan, at least, was prepared to go on the record on television explaining his own role in the Sizewell surveillance.

To return to the across-the-board denials of involvement in this surveillance by the relevant authorities, Zeus's own Articles of Association state that one of its objects is 'to carry on business, as security experts and agents of all kinds and to provide advisory and consultancy services to Government and other Authorities and to encourage the adoption of security and precautionary measures and devices against industrial and other espionage.'

While Zeus stated openly that it existed to provide advisory and consultancy services to 'Government and other Authorities', the government has remained extremely coy at revealing exactly what this relationship has been. During months of intensive questioning in the House of Commons throughout 1988 and 1989, government spokesmen consistently stonewalled.

A few examples will suffice. On 23 May 1988, Labour MP Ken Livingstone asked Defence spokesman Tim Sainsbury what payments had been made by his department each year from 1980 to date to Zeus and Lynx private security companies, and what was the nature of the work they had undertaken. (Lynx, it may be remembered, was the agency run by Jeremy Wetherall, who also played a leading role with Zeus.) Sainsbury replied, 'I am not aware that the MoD has had any dealings with either of the companies quoted.'[1]

Next Livingstone asked the Foreign Secretary what payments *his* department had made to Zeus and Lynx between 1980 and the present time, and the nature of the work undertaken. Replying on the Foreign Secretary's behalf, David Mellor said, 'The Foreign and Commonwealth Office has employed Zeus but not the Lynx security company. Detailed information on this subject is not kept in a centralised form and can only be researched at disproportionate cost.' However, he did reveal the one piece of information that has emerged in the House of Commons regarding Zeus: that the company had been used twice in 1983 for unspecified tasks.[2]

A year later, in February 1989, Labour MP Stanley Cohen asked the Secretary of State for the Home Office if he would list all his department's contracts with Zeus and Securipol (the subsidiary set up to dump nuclear waste) since 1979 and if he would give the purpose of each contract; to which the then Home Secretary Douglas Hurd replied that he could not do so, since 'records are only readily available from 1984' and they did not include contracts with either agency.

After weeks of similar answers, on 4 April 1989 Ken Livingstone asked for names of all private security firms employed by the government from 1979 onwards, the total costs involved and details of the duties performed by Zeus in 1982 and 1983, to which Tim Eggar, on behalf of the government, replied, 'Detailed information on this subject is not readily available and could be provided only at disproportionate cost.'[3] The only slender admission that Zeus has ever acted for the government has been Mellor's statement in 1988.

The recent 'greater openness' about our intelligence services is largely cosmetic, consisting as it does of admitting finally that not only MI5 but MI6 actually exist, publishing the names of those in charge of them and a rough estimate of the number of employees, and announcing that with the ending of the Cold War one of the main tasks of MI5 is intelligence gathering to assist in the fight against the IRA: no big deal. Our intelligence services still remain unaccountable, freed from the restrictions felt necessary in most of the rest of the industrialised world.

We know even less about the shadowy private network. How many of them are there, what are they used for and why? The opposition to Sizewell was a legitimate activity, openly carried out in a supposed democracy. It was scandalous and outrageous that those involved should be the target of a major surveillance operation. Who decided that they be monitored and who selected Zeus?

If, as Brian Crozier has said,[4] Margaret Thatcher was so interested in his own undercover set-up that she actually attended the founding meeting of Shield and allowed him open access to her at Chequers when she became Prime Minister, it must at least be possible that the surveillance was ordered at the highest level and by an agency which, because of the make-up of its board, was felt to be not only trustworthy but politically correct.

The Belgrano *Cover Up*

I played only one important part in the original researches into the Murrell murder. Having failed to discover anything either in what Robert Green told me or in Hilda's research into nuclear waste that would have made her such a threat that some kind of intelligence operation was mounted, and following further questioning, I made the connection between what appeared to be his work during the Falklands conflict and the sinking of the *Belgrano*.

Nothing that has happened since has changed my mind that it was the *Belgrano* leaks that inadvertently led to Hilda's murder. Major unanswered questions stand out. What exactly was decided at that panic meeting at 10 Downing Street on 19 March? Was a representative of the intelligence services present? And why did some 'informed sources' decide to 'leak' to the media that the *Conqueror* log had gone missing in such a way that the impression was given that it had been filched by a member of the submarine's crew, an impression so strong that the *Mail*, who decided to run with it, involved itself in a costly libel action? That decision was taken in the full knowledge that the log was in Washington.

It is against this background of mistrust, therefore, that we must set the information which Triona Guthrie passed on to Gary Murray in all good faith; information that West Mercia Police are convinced was the product of a malcontent's fevered imagination.

Had definite proof not become available, what kind of a reception would any journalist have had for suggesting that Sizewell protesters were under surveillance? Or that the surveillance was being masterminded by a private investigative agency with the unlikely name of Zeus?

If Zeus exists, then why not Ceres? Triona Guthrie's informant did not stop with the story of a supposed operation to break into Hilda Murrell's house and search it, based on information gleaned from a 1989 newspaper article. He also alleged that Ceres had provided in the north of England, particularly in Yorkshire, both surveillance and *agents provocateurs* (one of whom was Gricewith) during the 1984 miners' strike and that the latter had been responsible for some of the most notorious and violent incidents; that Hilda Murrell's death was not the only one that could be laid at their door.

If Hilda Murrell was not murdered for fifty pounds and a

handful of small items by an opportunist thief with masturbatory fantasies, then who is likely ever to admit that the
break-in had been carried out by freelance employees of yet
another shady agency? Certainly not those who employed the
agency in the first place.

Since Hilda Murrell's murder there have been a number of
violent deaths caused by opportunist burglars, often very young
men and for very small gain. Men and women in their eighties,
even their nineties, have been so attacked with the blame
variously apportioned to our having become a more violent
society and the growing need for such people to fund a drug
habit. But even given that such attacks were far rarer ten years
ago and crime directly related to drugs much lower, there is no
other single case of a burglar, after such a break-in, abducting
the victim and undertaking what even the West Mercia Police
agreed at the inquest to have been a systematic search of the
house. If West Mercia Police really have held the answer to all
this in their incident room since 1984, then ten years on it is
more than time they revealed it.

Like all notorious murder cases, that of Hilda Murrell has
produced its crop of oddballs and weird theories and is likely
to go on doing so. The true identity of Jack the Ripper
has continued to be 'revealed' for over a hundred years with
'certain proof' pointing to a whole range of people, from
a deranged member of the Royal Family, through the pai-
nter Walter Sickert, to an anonymous member of the Free-
masons.

The Murrell murder has taken an obsessive hold on some of
those closely involved. This is neither surprising nor unusual
in relatives and close friends of a victim, indeed it is understandable, particularly when time passes and a murderer is
still not caught or a miscarriage of justice remains unexposed.
There have been other recent examples, including Ron Smith,
father of the nurse, Helen Smith, raped and murdered in Saudi
Arabia; Jim Swire, whose daughter died in the Pan-Am bomb

disaster over Lockerbie; and the families of the Guildford Four and Birmingham Six.

Ron Smith drove everyone mad, including those of us who sought to help him. His belief that his daughter had died in deeply suspicious circumstances and that the Foreign Office appeared to have colluded in a cover-up to avoid embarrassing the Saudi government received short shrift from most of the media and very definitely from all the authorities concerned. His dogged refusal to give up or to accept what he was told, including being informed that he could not apply to have the inquest on his daughter held back home in Leeds, led to his being treated as a crazed obsessive, an object of derision. In the end, of course, he was triumphantly vindicated and proved to have been right all along. The official post mortems had, it seems, failed to show what was immediately apparent to the independent pathologist: that Helen Smith had been brutally raped before death.

In the *Independent* feature which had, we are told, inspired a disgruntled prisoner to concoct so detailed a scenario, Amanda Mitchison describes the effect the murder of his aunt has had on the person most closely involved, Robert Green: 'For more than five years he has lived in an atmosphere of heightened fear and excitement. He is obsessed with Hilda's murder and the long, dark exploration will lead him either to oblivion or – worse still – to a culprit. If this happened, would he ever recover from the sense of anti-climax? What would he do next? Would his anti-nuclear campaigning lose some of his zeal? Victory can be the greatest danger for this type of quest. Like the shark hunter who finds his quarry, Rob's identity, his sense of purpose, everything he stands for, may just "softly and suddenly vanish, and never be met with again".' Since the article appeared in 1989 Green's marriage has broken up. He must, however, remember that at the end of the day Ron Smith, against all the odds, was proved to have been right.

I do not consider myself to be a Murrell obsessive. My first attempt to research the story led to a good many unpleasant experiences and proved deeply frustrating, but life moves on. There were many worrying and disturbing stories before Hilda's murder and there have been plenty since. Years later I wrote a play surmising what might have happened, one of two around a theme I find fascinating: what happens when an awkward and uncompromising individual runs up against the power of the state? The second had as its protagonist that gay Cambridge spy and early employee of our intelligence services, Christopher Marlowe. It is hardly a new theme – Sophocles got there first with *Antigone*.

But Hilda's murder has remained unfinished business and it was tempting, in the light of the new information from Triona Guthrie and subsequent investigations by a number of interested colleagues, to look in more detail and with hindsight at the events surrounding her death and to examine and, where possible, corroborate that new information.

After researching the new evidence, interviewing a wide variety of people, examining material in the possession of colleagues and speaking to two extremely confidential sources with knowledge of events at the time, my own view remains diametrically opposed to that of West Mercia Police.

This is that accelerating panic over leaks of information to Tam Dalyell culminated on 19 March 1984, when the government was faced with a set of questions proving that he held precise information. As a result the special committee set up to look into leaks activated a series of urgent measures in a last-ditch attempt to track down the source and that every possibility was considered, however remote.

This resulted in a number of searches being carried out including that of Ravenscraoft and that in the case of Hilda Murrell, a soft target, a freelance unit was used. As I was finishing this book, I had it on the authority of a senior MI5 operative, now retired, that this was indeed the case and that during the operation two men, left alone in the house, 'seem to have gone berserk when the lady unexpectedly returned home'.

According to this source, the MI5 handler or liaison officer was severely castigated for the ensuing mess.

While West Mercia Police have discredited Triona Guthrie's information to their own satisfaction, in the light of this it is worth briefly recapping what she was told: that a freelance team, an offshoot of an agency often used by the intelligence services and code-named Ceres, was sent to Shrewsbury to search Hilda Murrell's house. One man, Team Member 1, did not enter the property but remained in the vicinity. A team of four, led by David Gricewith, and comprising Team Member 2, Spengler and Gricewith's girlfriend, then broke into the property and that the assault on Hilda Murrell took place while Gricewith and the woman were at Llanymynech searching the Shack. She was also told that it was the girlfiend, not Hilda, who was driven away in the car and that Hilda's body was dumped in an area known as Little America until it was moved to the copse at Hunkington – but I have found no way of confirming these latter pieces of information. After the event, the professionals moved in to organise the cover-up and I will only add that the MI5 source greeted with some amusement the West Mercia Police statement that they had been shown the relevant files and that there was no trace of any such operation.

Also, it is only necessary to read the *Independent* feature to see at once that it would not have been possible to base the story told to Triona Guthrie entirely on that.

What has also come to light, apart from the strange manner of his death, is that David Gricewith was an object of interest to a number of bodies. He appears to have been something quite other than the apparently reckless armed robber he was made out to be at his inquest, when just about every unsolved violent crime in West Yorkshire and beyond for the last seventeen years was attributed to him even though he had never previously been brought to court for any such activity.

To return, finally, to the matter of the *Belgrano* leaks, it also appears that at some point, for whatever reason, it was deliberately decided to muddy the waters by leaking spurious information as to the fate of the *Conqueror* log.

Speaking in the House of Lords on 2 March 1994 about another controversial issue – the possibility that arms were traded for aid to build the Pergau dam in Malaysia – Conservative peer Jim Prior, himself an ex-Thatcher Minister, defending a deal which he said had helped to save British jobs, castigated the press for criticising it. However, he also said that he had always thought in the eighties that 'large sections of the press were sycophantic to the Conservative government – frankly, they allowed the Thatcher government to get away with murder on a number of occasions'.[5]

In the case of Hilda Murrell that might well be true. But from what has come to light since, I do believe that as more and more information emerged on the sinking of the *Belgrano*, a decision was taken at the highest level to seek out as a matter of extreme urgency who was leaking it; and that also, for reasons unknown, the waters were deliberately muddied with the false trail of the *Conqueror* log. The search for possible documentary evidence was then passed on to a number of the agencies used by the government and the intelligence services and, at the end of the chain and the bottom of the heap, was a sleazy outfit, very possibly that described to Triona Guthrie, which broke into Ravenscroft.

No doubt other groups or single operatives made other searches which did not lead on to disaster so we will never know how widespread was the activity. Hilda Murrell's killer has never been found and, at the time of writing, can be fairly said to have got away with it. The subsequent cover-up might also be described as getting away with murder.

Notes

Chapter 1

1 *Hilda Murrell's Nature Notes*, ed. Sinker, Collins 1985.
2 Conversation with author.

Chapter 2

1 Murray, *Enemies of the State*, Simon & Schuster 1993.
  And in conversation with other sources.
2 Information from Robert Green. See Judith Cook, *Who Killed Hilda Murrell?*, NEL 1985.
3 *Ibid.*
4 West Mercia Police statement at inquest, December 1984.
5 Conversation with author.
6 *Ibid.*
7 Research John Osmond, HTV.
8 *Ibid.*
9 Statements made to journalists.
10 Conversation with author.
11 *Ibid.*
12 Conversation with author and Tam Dalyell, 1985.
13 Murray, *Enemies of the State*.
14 West Mercia Police statement, 26.3.84.
  'Rose Expert Is Murdered', *Shropshire Star*, 26.3.84.
15 Murray, *Enemies of the State*.

189

Chapter 3

1 All forensic information taken from inquest, December 1984.
2 *Ibid.*
3 *Ibid.*
4 *Shropshire Star*, 27.3.84.
5 *Ibid.*, 30.3.84.
6 *Ibid.*
7 'Profile of Killer', *Shropshire Star*, 6.4.84.
8 West Mercia Police press release, 19.4.84.
Conflicting reports in media immediately afterwards.
Conversation with author, September 1984.
Inquest evidence, December 1984.

Chapter 4

1 In conversation with her friends.
2 *Accident at Chelyabinsk*, Zhores Medvedev, Spokesman 1977.
3 To author and many others. See *Who Killed Hilda Murrell?*
4 Undated letter to Tam Dalyell.
5 Conversation with author.
6 *Ibid.*
7 Murray, *Enemies of the State* and others.
8 West Mercia Police press release, 12.9.84.
Central TV, 12.9.84.
9 *Hansard*, 9.1.85.
10 Major West Mercia Police press release, January 1985.

Chapter 5

1 Hugo Young, *One of Us*, Pan 1991.
2 Ian Gilmour, *Dancing with Dogma*, Simon & Schuster 1992.
3 *New Statesman*, 17.8.84.
4 Peter Wright, *Spycatcher*, Viking 1987.
5 Sanity, August 1986.

Chapter 6

1 *Nuclear Power*, Walter G. Patterson. 2nd ed. London 1985.
2 *Ibid.*

3 'Thatcher War on Peace Studies', *Guardian* 16.10.93.

4 'Trail of Clues for the Sizewell Sleuth', *Guardian* 28.1.85.

5 *Who's Who*, 1992.

6 Published letter to the Prime Minister, 25.1.89.

7 *Ibid.*

8 *Hansard*, 23.5.88. Cols 27/28.

9 Correspondence from private source.

10 *Ibid.*

11 *Observer*, 17.1.85.
   Daily Mirror, February 1985.
   World in Action, 4.3.85.
   Judith Cook, *Who Killed Hilda Murrell?*, June 1985.

12 Correspondence from private source.

13 *Ibid.*

14 *Observer*, 27.1.85.

15 'Send in the Snoops', *Shropshire Star*, 14.6.85.

16 Conversation with author.

Chapter 7

1 Ian Gilmour, *Dancing with Dogma*. London 1992, pp. 298/299.

2 *Ibid.*

3 Hugo Young, *One of Us*. London 1993 ed., pp. 262/3.

4 *Hansard*, 31.3.82.

5 Clive Ponting, *The Right to Know*. London 1985, pp. 86/7. Ponting argues that Lewin wanted an all-out naval war and all vessels to be sunk without warning; he asks if the Cabinet knew that the *Belgrano* had been recalled but decided to sink her regardless.

6 *Hansard*, 4.5.93.

7 *Ibid.*

8 Conversations with author.

9 *Ibid.*

10 It was entirely fortuitous that I noticed Green's Falklands citation for his services during the campaign. I then questioned him about it.

Chapter 8

1 *Shropshire Star*, 29.3.84 and subsequently.

2 Conversation with author, January 1985.

3 *Evening Standard*, 7.2.85.

4 Conversation with author, March 1984.
  Also Graham Smith, *Death of a Rose-grower*. London 1985.
5 *Hansard*, 26.5.85.
6 Letter from Brittan to Gerald Kaufman, 17.6.1986.
7 Police press release, 26.3.84.
8 Inquest transcript, 5.12.84.
9 *Ibid.*
10 *Ibid.*

Chapter 9

1 Clive Ponting, *The Right to Know*, Sphere Books 1985.
2 *Ibid.*
3 *Ibid.* and following.

Chapter 10

1 *Sunday Times*, 6.1.85.
2 Letter in possession of author.
3 Conversation with author.
4 *Hansard*, 17.1.85.
5 Letter shown to author.
6 *Shropshire Star*, 28.1.85.
7 *Ibid*, 29.1.85.
8 Conversation with author.
  Guardian 21.2.85.
9 Conversation with Graham Smith – *Death of a Rose-grower*, London 1985.
10 *Daily Telegraph*, 16.6.85.

Chapter 11

1 Copies of letters in author's possession.
2 Brian Crozier, *Free Agent*. London 1993.
3 *Ibid.*
4 *Ibid.*
5 Gary Murray, *Enemies of the State*, London 1993 and also checked out from informed sources after publication of the book.
6 Conversation with barrister.
7 *Ibid.*

NOTES

Chapter 12

1 Conversation with author.
2 *Ibid.* and following information.
3 The 'core story' is an amplified version of the affidavit given in *Enemies of the State*, following further investigation, interviews etc. by, as well as Gary Murray, myself and journalistic colleagues.
4 *Yorkshire Post*, 27.1.88.
5 *Ibid.*
6 *Enemies of the State.*
7 Catriona Guthrie's affidavit.

Chapter 13

1 (i) Researcher to MP.
  (ii) James Rusbridger.
2 *Yorkshire Post*, 27.1.88.
3 *Ibid.*
4 *Enemies of the State.*
5 *The Times*, 8.9.88.
  Yorkshire Post, 8.9.88.
6 Inquest report.
7 *Ibid.*
8 *Ibid.*
9 *Ibid.*
10 *Ibid.*
11 *Ibid.*
12 *The Times*, 27.1.88.
  Yorkshire Post, 27.1.88.
  Daily Telegraph, 27.1.88.
  Daily Express, 27.1.88.
13 *The Times*, 22.1.88 and 23.1.88.
14 *Daily Telegraph*, 7.9.88.
15 *Ibid.*
16 *Enemies of the State* and questioning by author.
17 Confidential but bona fide source.

Chapter 14

1 Tape recording of press conference with author.

2 Copies with author.
3 West Mercia detective in conversation with researcher, March 1990.

Chapter 15

1 Chapman Pincher, *Their Trade is Treachery*. London 1981.
2 Hugo Young, *One of Us*.
3 The Westland affair has been well documented. One of the best and most detailed accounts can be found in Hugo Young's *One of Us* and a succinct and brief one in Gilmour's *Dancing with Dogma*.
4 *The Thatcher Factor*, Channel 4, 6.4.89.

Chapter 16

1 *Hansard*, 23.5.88.
2 *Ibid*.
3 *Hansard*, 4.4.89.
4 Brian Crozier, *Free Agent*. London 1993.
5 *World at One*, BBC Radio 4, 3.3.94.
Guardian, 3.3.94.

Bibliography

Cook, Judith, *Who Killed Hilda Murrell?* London: New English Library, 1985.

Crozier, Brian, *Free Agent*. London: Harper Collins, 1993.

Gavshon, Arthur & Rice, Desmond, *The Sinking of the Belgrano*. London: New English Library, 1984.

Gilmour, Ian, *Dancing with Dogma*. London: Simon & Schuster, 1992.

Harris, Robert, *Gotcha! – The Media, the Government and the Falklands War*. London: Faber & Faber, 1985.

Medvedev, Zhores, *Accident at Chelyabinsk*. London: Angus and Robertson, 1977.

Murray, Gary, *Enemies of the State*. London: Simon & Schuster, 1993.

Norton-Taylor, R., *In Defence of the Realm*. London: Hogarth Press, 1991.

Patterson, Walter, *Nuclear Power*, 2nd ed. London: Penguin Books, 1983.

Ponting, Clive, *The Right to Know*. London: Sphere, 1985.

Smith, Graham, *Death of a Rosegrower*. London: Cecil Woolf, 1985.

Wright, Peter, *Spycatcher*, NY ed.: Viking, 1987.

Young, Hugo, *One of Us*, final ed. London: Pan Macmillan, 1991.

Index

196

INDEX

INDEX

199